A Taste of Aloha

A Collection of Recipes
from
The Junior League of Honolulu

The purpose of the Junior League is exclusively educational and charitable. The organization's aims are to promote voluntarism, to develop the potential of its members for voluntary participation in community affairs and to demonstrate the effectiveness of trained volunteers.

Copyright 1983

First Printing	September, 1983	20,000 copies
Second Printing	February, 1981	30,000 copies
Third Printing	July, 1986	12,000 copies
Fourth Printing	March, 1988	10,000 copies
Fifth Printing	May, 1989	15,000 copies
Sixth Printing	April, 1991	10,000 copies
Seventh Printing*	November, 1993	20,000 copies
Eighth Printing*	February, 1994	36,000 copies

(*Southern Living® **Hall of Fame** edition)

The Junior League of Honolulu, Inc.
A Taste of Aloha
1802-A Keeaumoku Street
Honolulu, Hawaii 96822

ISBN 0-9612484-0-8

Foreword

Hawaii is a colorful panorama of cultures, providing a vast and unique display of culinary delights. Our islands are blessed with a wide array of fresh seafood, crisp vegetables and luscious fruits. Complementing these are Oriental spices, European flair and Yankee ingenuity.

Many of our recipes are family favorites, handed down through generations. Others have arrived in the islands with each new wave of settlers. All are suited to our relaxed island lifestyle and represent the varied influence of a wide world of cultures.

Our recipes have been tested for quality and edited for clarity and consistency. The glossary at the back of the book will acquaint you with new cooking ingredients and methods of preparation. These words are noted throughout the book with asterisks (*). A fish chart will clarify our local names for various fish.

And now...

A Taste Of Aloha

Table of
Of
Contents

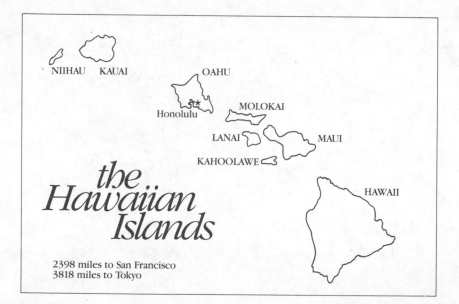

NIIHAU KAUAI   OAHU

                          MOLOKAI
        Honolulu

              LANAI   MAUI

        KAHOOLAWE

the
Hawaiian
Islands   HAWAII

2398 miles to San Francisco
3818 miles to Tokyo

Historic Background

In the beginning, there was the sea. Nothing has so influenced life in Hawaii as the sea has. Our islands were born from the sea, heaved from the ocean bottom by volcanic eruption for more than 40 million years. They emerged slowly, the most isolated island chain in the world.

Not until about 1,000 years ago, in the great voyaging canoes from the South Pacific, did man discover Hawaii. The canoes of the voyagers were double hulled and high-prowed to move through high seas. The hulls were made from hollowed logs felled with stone axes. A platform was built between the two hulls for the women and children because these travelers were not simply exploring—they were migrating as a people to a new land.

The steersmen were guided by the navigator who found his way by the stars, the ocean swells, the cloud patterns that formed over land, the drifting debris and the seasonal flights of birds. They had no written language. They needed none.

The men chosen for these perilous voyages were strong and muscular, of great endurance, and by today's athletic standards, often grossly overweight. Fat was cultivated before a voyage because it could sustain the traveler through periods of rationed food and water and because it would insulate the body against sharp ocean winds.

Food was a major concern of the ancient voyagers, not only for the sea journey itself but as a source of crops to sustain them after landfall. Cages were built into the hulls of the canoes to hold chickens and pigs brought for breeding stock. Plants for crops— taro, coconut, banana, breadfruit and sweet potatoes—were carefully tended on the passage so that they would root in the new land. Dried fish, dried bananas, taro, yams and breadfruit were stowed beneath the deck and in the hulls as food for the long voyage. Fresh water was carried in lengths of bamboo and oiled gourds, and fish were hooked with carved pieces of shell or bone.

For 400 years, the voyaging canoes traveled between Hawaii and Tahiti, and then for reasons not entirely understood, the great migration ceased. These early voyagers named our islands, mountains and harbors and the deep sea channels between the islands. Southwest of Maui is the channel they named *Kealaikahiki. Ke ala*—the path. *I kahiki*—to Tahiti. This was the route to the homeland of the early Hawaiians.

On the long canoe voyages and during the first days in the new land, the Hawaiian people knew and dreaded hunger. Food was precious, feasting was a religious as well as a social event.

The Hawaiian chief claimed plots of land running from the top of the tall mountains through the valley to the edge of the sea, a wedge-shaped parcel called an *ahupua'a*. Each *ahupua'a* could produce most of the things its people needed. There were the high forests for wood, the flat land for the taro patches, the seashore for the fishponds and the ocean beyond as a vast store of edible seaweed and 600 kinds of tropical fish.

The growing plants that had been so carefully nurtured with precious fresh drinking water on the long sea voyages flourished in this warm and sunny place. The fisherman living at the seashore took his fish into the valley where he was given *poi*, vegetables and fruit. This constant exchange explains the diet that so well nourished these people, a handsome and healthy race. Thus they lived, these early settlers, in the bright sun and the warm rains of a land that was kind to them. Their plants flourished, their pigs grew fat.

Their language had many words for food and eating but none at all for time. They were isolated by thousands of miles of open sea from a world where famine and war and disease prevailed. They prayed to their gods, they shared with each other and they were secure.

The fertility of the land was conserved, and here where there was no gold or silver, fresh water was wealth. A chief's wealth was measured by the water his village controlled. The farmer needed fresh water to irrigate his taro patch because taro provided his daily food—the pounded paste from the root of the taro called *poi*.

The other essential in the Hawaiian diet was fish. Many were caught from the sea but others were cultivated in great walled-in sea ponds. Carefully fitted stones of coral were piled up to form the seawall and a sluice gate was built from heavy timber at the opening. The high tide would bring in the fish, the gate would be closed and the fish were trapped.

Food was cooked in an *'imu*, a shallow pit dug into the ground. In the hole a fire was lighted and rocks were heated almost red-hot. Banana leaves were laid over the rocks and the food cooked there. Most food, though, was eaten cold from bowls made of native wood. These *poi* bowls are now treasured among the precious works of art left by the early Hawaiians.

The major time of feasting was the *Makahiki*, a time of games and contests begun with prayers to the god Lono for rain and abundant crops. Lono was represented by a staff surmounted by a figurehead of a man. Below this was a crossbar from which hung a sheet of white tapa. So on a January morning in 1778 when such a mast and white sails were sighted off Kauai, it was apparent to the Hawaiians that Lono had returned. It was on that morning that the ship bearing the British explorer, Captain James Cook, appeared and ended forever Hawaii's isolation.

The Hawaiians greeted Captain Cook as the god Lono, but because humans rarely behave as gods are expected to, Cook failed the Hawaiians. A mutual misunderstanding led to a fight and Cook died from wounds on a beach on the island of Hawaii at Kealakekua Bay.

Hawaii had been re-discovered, and soon became a wintering

place for foreign ships and the thousands of men in their crews. The ships brought new livestock, and new fruit trees and garden vegetables were introduced from their stores.

But one of the most remarkable changes in their way of life was created by the Hawaiians themselves. To the distress of the chiefs, in 1819, Liholiho, heir of Kamehameha the Great, was persuaded to give a public feast at which men and women ate together. This act had been forbidden since the days of the great migration and had now wiped out their traditional religious system. But it was to be replaced by another.

Christianity was brought to Hawaii by a small party of young evangelical Protestants who came to Hawaii in 1820 from Puritan New England to "convert the heathens." The Hawaiians were friendly to the newcomers, bringing presents of fresh pork, corn, beans, goats' milk and bananas. The missionaries accepted chickens as fees for performing the Christian rites of marriage and burial.

From the beginning, the missionaries enjoyed a cordial relation-ship with the Hawaiian monarchy, one that linked Hawaii to the United States. At a time when England and France were anxious to annex the Hawaiian kingdom, Hawaii remained independent, until the United States itself annexed the faraway kingdom.

In terms of time, the kingdom of Hawaii was a brief interlude in the long history of the Pacific. From the time that Kamehameha the Great united all the major islands except Kauai in 1795 until Queen Liliuokalani was imprisoned on the upper floor of her palace in 1895 and the kingdom had ended forever, Hawaii moved from a stone age culture to a European-style monarchy. The ogre in the fairy tale was change—it came too quickly without understanding or acceptance.

Kamehameha was a unique man, a military genius and a political strategist, commanding an army that fought with spears and a king-dom coveted by the great powers of the day. He died in 1819 and his bones are said to be buried in a lost sea cave, perhaps in his own war canoe as the great chiefs before him were.

The kings who succeeded him moved rapidly into the civilization of the time, occasionally with dire results. Kamehameha II and his wife died in London in 1825 of the measles, a disease which had never been introduced to Hawaii and for which they had no immunity. Kamehameha III died childless and the throne next went to Prince Alexander Liholiho. His wedding to Emma Rooke was followed by a great ball at the palace, the first of many European-influenced parties the couple would give.

One of these is described in the diary of British visitor Sophia Cracroft. "Dinner served in the throne room of the palace to our surprise was as well-appointed as it would have been in London." There was a proper English butler (although Sophie suspected that he drank) and at each plate a printed menu listing eleven courses.

The last king of Hawaii was Kalakaua. He and Queen Kapiolani built the present Iolani Palace, and it was there that their coronation was held in 1883. They entertained on a lavish scale. This was a time of dinners in the royal boathouse, picnics in the mountains of Nuuanu, elaborate visits to the outer islands and great house parties at country estates.

Time was running out though, not only for the portly king but for the kingdom. Kalakaua died in 1891 and his sister Liliuokalani was proclaimed queen. Two years later, a revolution backed by Americans planning to annex the kingdom removed Liliuokalani from the throne. She was arrested and imprisoned for nearly eight months in two second floor rooms of Iolani Palace. It was there that she is thought to have transcribed the music to her poignant composition, "*Aloha Oe*," translated as "Farewell to Thee." It is a song of parting, the end of a unique century and a gentle kingdom.

The story of Hawaii, though, is far more than that of the Hawaiians and the Americans. The history of Hawaii is a rainbow of all the races who have come here with their own customs and traditions and have made Hawaii a more interesting place for all of us.

By the mid 1840's, small groups of Chinese had migrated to the islands and had leased farmland. In 1851, the first boatload of Chinese laborers recruited to work on the sugar plantations arrived in Hawaii.

But the same qualities of industriousness, frugality and willingness to venture that their employers so admired, moved the Chinese off the plantations as soon as their contracts expired. They managed to save enough money from their $36 annual wages to open stores or start farms.

In the rainbow arched valleys, on the dusty plains below the green mountains and in the swamps of Waikiki they raised chickens and ducks and cultivated vegetables from the seeds they brought from China. They introduced water chestnuts, litchi (lychee), mandarin oranges, mustard cabbage and the delectable dwarf Chinese banana.

Chinese cooperatives grew coffee, peanuts and bananas, and this cooperative system eventually evolved into the *hui*, an organization of small investors who together have built banks, stores and development companies. These *huis* have founded several great fortunes among the Chinese-Americans living in Hawaii.

As the Chinese left the plantations, the Japanese were brought here on contracts to replace them. The first great wave of immigration came in 1886, made up of tenant farmers from southern Japan who were facing starvation after successive crop failures.

They preserved their traditions, and spent as little money as possible for food since it was being saved either to return to Japan or to become independent of the plantation. Some of the workers agreed to work an extra half-hour each day for the use of a quarter-acre of land on which to grow vegetables. They cultivated soy beans, daikon, turnips, eggplant and cabbage.

The plantation housing, as their own had been in Japan, was without ovens. Food was boiled, broiled, fried or steamed. The principal seasoning, still indispensable in the Japanese kitchen, was shoyu or soy sauce. Made of soy beans, barley and salt, it is used to flavor everything from sashimi to tempura. The presentation of Japanese food is as important as the menu itself, and the exquisite lacquer and ceramic bowls and trays used to serve each dish are treasured by collectors.

The Koreans arrived in the islands at the turn of the century, again as contract laborers, planning to save and return to the Hermit Kingdom. But when Japan annexed Korea in 1910, they abandoned the dream of going home. A pungent pickled cabbage known as Kim Chee and spicy marinated beef, Kalbi, are just two of the Korean dishes added to our island heritage.

With Hawaii's annexation as a territory in 1900, Asians could no longer become naturalized citizens under United States law, forcing the sugar planters to look elsewhere for potential laborers. From Madeira and the Azores came the Portuguese, bringing with them the Catholic religion, the *ukulele* ("jumping flea") and the dominant strain of "pidgin" English used today. These newcomers greatly affected Hawaii's culture, contributing far more than Portuguese bean soup, malasadas and sweet bread to the ethnic flavor of these islands.

The next and last large migration to the sugar fields came from the Philippines. An industrious and artistic people, their fiestas and Spanish-influenced traditions added another flavor to the foods of Hawaii.

Most recently arrived in the islands are the refugees from war and political oppression in Southeast Asia; families from Thailand, Viet Nam and Cambodia who frequently have escaped with little more than they could carry. The earliest Hawaiians in their great canoes, after all, arrived in much the same way.

Hawaii has offered a warm welcome to all of us, all migrants who have come here intentionally or by chance, to give of what we know and to borrow from others. In a place where we are all minorities, we have learned to look for the best of what each has brought here, to understand our similarities and to appreciate our differences.

Lois Taylor

King Protea

Appetizers and Pupus

Crispy Won Ton

Makes 8 dozen

3/4 pound	ground pork
6	fresh shrimp, finely chopped
6	water chestnuts,* finely chopped
2	green onions, finely chopped
2 tablespoons	chopped Chinese parsley*
2	eggs, slightly beaten
1 teaspoon	salt
1 small clove	garlic, diced
96	won ton pi squares*
3 cups	vegetable oil

Combine first 8 ingredients in a bowl or food processor. Mix well. Place approximately 1 teaspoon of mixture in center of the won ton square. Fold square diagonally to make a triangle and seal the edges with water. Heat vegetable oil in a skillet. Drop won ton in one at a time so they do not stick together. Cook until golden brown 1 to 1 1/2 minutes, turning if necessary. Drain on paper towels. Serve warm. If made ahead, store in paper bag and refrigerate. Heat in oven before serving for crispy product. Serve with Soy and Hot Mustard Dipping Sauce or Sweet Sour Sauce (see index).

General Poon's Pupu
Serves 6

2 tablespoons	vegetable oil
4 cloves	garlic, crushed
1 pound	beef tenderloin, finely chopped
1 tablespoon	curry powder
1/2 cup	finely chopped celery
1/2 teaspoon	salt
1/2 teaspoon	Maggi seasoning
	lettuce leaves
	mint leaves

Heat oil and sauté garlic. Add meat, curry powder, celery and seasonings. Stir and cook for 5 minutes. Serve in a bowl surrounded by lettuce leaves. Put a spoonful of meat mixture into a lettuce leaf. Add a mint leaf, fold and eat. Note: This is excellent when entertaining a small group.

Teriyaki Sausage
Serves 10

2 pounds	mild or hot Portuguese sausage*
3/4 cup	soy sauce
1 1/4 cups	sugar
1 tablespoon	chopped fresh ginger*

Cut Portuguese sausage into 1/4-inch slices. Combine remaining ingredients in a saucepan. Add sausage and simmer for 35 minutes. Serve hot with toothpicks.

Boneless
Chicken Pupus

5 pounds	boneless chicken thighs
4 tablespoons	rice flour*
4 tablespoons	sugar
1/2 teaspoon	salt
5 tablespoons	soy sauce
2 tablespoons	chopped green onions
2	eggs, slightly beaten
1 – 2 cloves	garlic, minced
1 teaspoon	finely chopped fresh ginger*
	vegetable oil

Garnish: Pineapple chunks and sesame seeds

Skin chicken and cut into bite-size pieces. Combine rice flour, sugar, salt, soy sauce, onions, eggs, garlic and ginger. Marinate chicken in mixture for 2 hours, preferably overnight. Turn every few hours. Fry pieces in hot oil until brown and crisp. Drain. Garnish with pineapple chunks and sprinkle with sesame seeds. Serve hot or cold.

Lumpia
Serves 25

This well-loved Filipino dish is a tasty combination of ingredients neatly wrapped in a thin dough and deep fried.

1/2 pound	ground pork
1/2 pound	ground beef
1/2 cup	chopped onion
1/2 pound	raw shrimp, chopped
2	eggs, beaten
1/2 cup	chopped mushrooms
1/2 cup	grated carrot
1/4 cup	chopped green onion
2 cups	shredded won bok*
3 cloves	garlic, minced
2 tablespoons	soy sauce
	salt and pepper to taste
50	lumpia wrappers*
	milk
	vegetable oil

In a large skillet, sauté pork, beef and onion. Drain excess grease. Add shrimp to skillet and cook for 1 minute. Remove from heat. Add eggs, mushrooms, carrot, green onion, won bok, garlic, soy sauce, salt and pepper. Set aside to cool. Put a heaping tablespoon of cooled mixture on each lumpia wrapper. Roll up, forming a small cylinder. Tuck ends into roll and seal wrapper with milk. Deep fry in oil until brown. Note: Keep lumpia wrappers under a damp cloth. Lumpia wrappers will fall apart if mixture is not thoroughly cooled. Serve with Sweet Sour Lumpia Sauce (see index).

Mushroom Turnovers

Turnovers

8 ounces	cream cheese, softened
1/2 pound	butter
2 cups	sifted flour
1	egg yolk
2 teaspoons	Half and Half

Combine cheese and butter. Work in flour until a smooth dough is formed. Refrigerate for 2 hours. Make separate mixture of egg yolk and cream. Set aside.

Filling

1/2 pound	fresh mushrooms, sliced
1	onion, minced
3 tablespoons	butter
2 teaspoons	flour
1/2 teaspoon	salt
1 teaspoon	dill weed
1/2 cup	sour cream

Preheat oven to 375 degrees. Sauté mushrooms and onion in butter. Add flour and salt and cook for 2 minutes. Remove from heat. Stir in sour cream and dill. Roll dough 1/8 inch thick. Cut into 3-inch round circles. Place 1 teaspoon filling just off center of the dough. Fold and press edge together. Seal with fork tines. Paint with egg yolk and cream mixture. Bake for 15 to 20 minutes. Note: This recipe freezes well.

Börek

Makes 8 dozen

A Turkish recipe that can be used with a variety of different fillings.

Meat filling

1^1/$_2$ pounds	lean ground beef
^{1}/$_2$ cup	pine nuts
1^1/$_2$ cups	chopped onion
^{1}/$_2$ cup	chopped parsley
3 tablespoons	red wine vinegar
^{3}/$_4$ teaspoon	ground allspice
^{1}/$_4$-^{1}/$_2$ teaspoon	dill weed
	salt, pepper and cayenne to taste

In a large skillet, brown beef with pine nuts and onion. Add parsley, vinegar, allspice, cayenne, dill, salt and pepper. Set aside.

Cheese filling

10 ounces	feta cheese, crumbled
2	eggs, beaten
^{1}/$_4$ cup	chopped parsley

In a bowl, combine cheese, eggs and parsley. Set aside.

40 – 50	lumpia wrappers*
	milk

Cut lumpia wrappers in half. Keep wrappers under a damp cloth. Place a teaspoon of filling at one end of each wrapper. Roll up, forming a small cylinder. Tuck ends into roll and seal wrapper with milk. Deep fry until golden brown, drain and serve hot.

Kamaboko Tempura

Makes 40

A great hors d'oeuvre for a Japanese dinner.

¾ cup	flour
¾ teaspoon	salt
2 teaspoons	sugar
½ teaspoon	baking powder
¼ cup	water
6	eggs
¼ cup	minced green onion
1	kamaboko,* grated
	vegetable oil

Combine flour, salt, sugar and baking powder. Beat water and eggs together and add to flour mixture. Add green onions and kamaboko. Drop a teaspoon of mixture into hot oil (375 degrees) and deep fry until brown. Serve on a platter with Soy and Hot Mustard Dipping Sauce (see index).

Sweet and Sour Chicken Wings

Serves 12

5 pounds	chicken wings or drumettes
4	eggs, beaten
2 cups	cornstarch
1/2 cup	vegetable oil
2 teaspoons	garlic salt
1 teaspoon	freshly ground black pepper
1 teaspoon	salt

Preheat oven to 350 degrees. Cut each chicken wing into 3 sections. Reserve the wing tips to make stock. Dip the other chicken pieces in beaten eggs. Roll each piece in cornstarch and fry until golden brown. Transfer chicken to baking dishes. Mix garlic salt, pepper and salt together and sprinkle evenly over chicken.

Sauce

1/2 cup	chicken stock
1 cup	sugar
1 cup	cider vinegar
6 tablespoons	catsup
2 tablespoons	soy sauce
2 teaspoons	salt

Combine the ingredients and pour over chicken. Bake for 30 minutes. Note: This can be made up to 3 days ahead. Reheat before serving.

Paniolo
Macadamia Dip

8 ounces	cream cheese, softened
2 tablespoons	milk
1 (2½-ounce) jar	dried chipped beef, shredded
⅓ cup	finely chopped green pepper
½ teaspoon	garlic salt
¼ teaspoon	pepper
2 teaspoons	onion flakes
2 – 3 teaspoons	prepared horseradish
½ cup	sour cream
½ cup	coarsely chopped macadamia nuts *
2 teaspoons	butter

Preheat oven to 350 degrees. Combine cream cheese with milk, blending well. Add chipped beef, green pepper, seasonings, onion flakes and horseradish. Fold in sour cream. Spoon into a shallow baking dish. In a small frying pan, glaze the macadamia nuts in butter. Sprinkle nuts over cream cheese mixture. Bake for 20 minutes. Serve hot with crackers.

Sweet 'n Sour Meatballs

Serves 10

Meatballs

1 pound	lean ground beef
¾ cup	minced celery
¼ cup	chopped almonds
1 clove	garlic, minced
1 teaspoon	salt
½ cup	soft bread crumbs
1 teaspoon	soy sauce
2	eggs, slightly beaten
½ teaspoon	pepper

In a large bowl, thoroughly mix all ingredients. Form into small meatballs. Brown meatballs and drain on paper towels.

Sauce

1 cup	chicken bouillon
½ cup	sugar
3 tablespoons	cornstarch
½ cup	pineapple juice, reserved from pineapple chunks
½ cup	vinegar
2 tablespoons	soy sauce
1	green pepper, chopped
1 (8-ounce) can	pineapple chunks

In a saucepan, add bouillon, sugar, cornstarch, pineapple juice, vinegar and soy sauce. Over medium heat, stir for 3 minutes or until thickened. Add green pepper, pineapple chunks and meatballs. Simmer for 15 minutes.

Artichoke Fritatta   *Serves 8*

2 (6-ounce) jars	marinated artichoke hearts
1/2 cup	chopped onion
1 clove	garlic, minced
4	eggs, beaten
1/4 cup	bread crumbs
1/4 teaspoon	salt
1/8 teaspoon	pepper
1/8 teaspoon	oregano
1/8 teaspoon	chili powder
2 tablespoons	minced parsley
2 cups	grated sharp Cheddar cheese

Preheat oven to 325 degrees. Drain marinade from one jar of artichoke hearts into frying pan. Chop artichokes and set aside. Sauté onion and garlic in marinade. In a large bowl, mix eggs, bread crumbs, salt, pepper, oregano, chili powder and parsley. Stir in cheese. Add artichokes and onion-garlic mixture. Pour into a greased 7 x 11-inch pan. Bake for 30 minutes. Cool in pan and cut into bite-size pieces. Note: Best if served warm.

Baked Jalapeño Bean Dip

Makes 3 cups

8 ounces	cream cheese
1 pint	sour cream
1 (10^1/2-ounce) can	jalapeño bean dip
1 (1.5-ounce) package	taco seasoning mix
	Tabasco, to taste
6	green onions, thinly sliced
1/4 cup	shredded Cheddar cheese
1/4 cup	shredded Jack cheese

Combine cream cheese and sour cream in food processor. Add bean dip, seasoning mix and Tabasco. Process. Stir in onions. Place in a shallow baking dish and top mixture with Cheddar and Jack cheese. Bake at 350 degrees for 20 to 30 minutes. Serve with tortilla or corn chips.

Chinese Fishcake

Serves 6—8

1 pound	fishpaste*
1 tablespoon	cornstarch
4 tablespoons	chopped Chinese parsley*
4 tablespoons	chopped green onion
1 tablespoon	soy sauce
1 tablespoon	oyster sauce*
1/4 cup	diced water chestnuts* (optional)
	vegetable oil

Mix first seven ingredients together. Pour 1/2 inch of vegetable oil into frying pan. Drop 1 tablespoon of mixture into oil to make puffs or use 2 tablespoons for fish patties. Brown on one side and turn and flatten with spatula. Drain and serve hot.

29

Hawaiian Sesame Shrimp

Serves 8

1 tablespoon	sesame seeds
2 tablespoons	sesame oil*
2 tablespoons	vegetable oil
1 pound	medium shrimp, shelled and deveined
1/2 cup	chopped green onion
1/2 teaspoon	salt
1/4 teaspoon	pepper
1 tablespoon	brown sugar
1 tablespoon	soy sauce

Preheat oven to 300 degrees. Toast sesame seeds until golden brown. Heat oils in a heavy pan over high heat. Add shrimp, green onion, salt, pepper and sugar. Stir-fry for 1 to 3 minutes. Reduce heat to low, add soy sauce and stir. Remove from heat and sprinkle with sesame seeds. Serve hot.

Sashimi

Only the freshest salt-water fish should be used for sashimi.

cabbage, finely shredded
fresh ahi*
carrot, grated
daikon,* grated
parsley sprigs
finely minced fresh ginger*
lemon wedges

Cover the serving platter with cabbage. Skin and fillet fish. Cut fish fillets across the grain in 2-inch by 1-inch slices and about 1/4-inch thick. The fish must be kept very cold. Dip hands in cold water often while handling fish. Arrange fish slices in an overlapping pattern on top of shredded cabbage. Encircle the fish with grated carrot, daikon and parsley. Place lemon wedges, ginger and dipping sauces in separate bowls. Serve with Wasabi Dipping Sauce or Soy and Hot Mustard Dipping Sauce (see index).

Wasabi Dipping Sauce

4 teaspoons   wasabi* powder
1 1/2 teaspoons   water
soy sauce

Make a thick paste of wasabi and water. Place a dab of wasabi in soy or dipping dish and add soy sauce to taste. Serve with Sashimi (see index).

Kim Chee Dip
Serves 4—6

8 ounces cream cheese, softened
1/2 cup   chopped kim chee,* drained

In a food processor, combine cream cheese and kim chee and process until smooth. Chill. Serve with crackers or potato chips.

Marinated Mushrooms
Serves 6—8

Make in advance for a pupu or add to "Hawaiian Grab Bag."

2/3 cup olive oil
1/2 cup water
4 tablespoons lemon juice
1 bay leaf
6 peppercorns
2 cloves garlic, crushed
1/2 teaspoon salt
1 pound fresh mushrooms

Combine first seven ingredients in a skillet and bring to a boil. Reduce heat. Cover and simmer for 15 minutes. Strain and return the marinade to the skillet. Add the mushrooms and simmer for 5 minutes, stirring occasionally. Cool. Refrigerate in a covered container for 1 to 2 days. Serve with toothpicks.

Hawaiian
Grab Bag

Dressing

2¼ cups	mayonnaise
1⅓ cups	sour cream
⅓ cup	prepared horseradish
2 tablespoons	dry mustard
¾ teaspoon	Beau Monde
2 tablespoons	lemon juice
½ teaspoon	dill weed
½ teaspoon	freshly ground black pepper
1 teaspoon	garlic salt

Mix ingredients early in the day to enhance the flavor.

Grab Bag Ingredients

2 (8-ounce) cans	water chestnuts*
2	avocados, peeled, pitted and thickly sliced
1 pound	medium shrimp, cooked, shelled and deveined
2	green peppers, sliced in strips lengthwise
1 pint	cherry tomatoes
2	cucumbers, unpeeled, thickly sliced
1 pound	Marinated Mushrooms, drained

Just before serving, combine Grab Bag ingredients and marinated mushrooms. Add dressing and toss gently. Serve with toothpicks. Note: Mushrooms must be made 1 to 2 days in advance.

Hawaiian "Artichoke" Cocktail

Serves 12

An Island surprise.

3 breadfruit,* baseball size
2 cups Caesar salad dressing
1 egg, hard cooked
lettuce leaves

In a large pot, cover whole breadfruit with salted water and bring to a boil. Simmer for 1 hour and 45 minutes, keeping breadfruit submerged. Drain and cool. Peel, cut out centers and cut into bite-size pieces. Marinate overnight in Caesar dressing. Serve on a bed of lettuce and sprinkle with chopped egg. Note: Breadfruit must be very immature.

Albert Schmid
Executive Chef
Dillingham Corporation
Honolulu, Hawaii

Stuffed Lychee

Makes 3 dozen

2 (20-ounce) cans whole seedless lychee,* drained
8 ounces cream cheese, softened
2¹/2 ounces crystalized ginger, finely chopped
*Garnish: Chopped macadamia nuts**

Combine cream cheese and ginger. Stuff mixture into lychee with small spoon, butter knife or a pastry bag. Chill. Garnish and serve.

Anchovy Stuffed Olives

Serves 4 — 6

Even people who don't like anchovies like this.

1 (2-ounce) tin	anchovy fillets
1 (2-ounce) jar	pimientos, minced
$1/3$ cup	red wine vinegar
1 tablespoon	olive oil
1 clove	garlic, minced
1 (6-ounce) can	pitted medium black olives
$1/4$ cup	minced parsley

Drain anchovy oil into a bowl. Stir in pimientos, vinegar, olive oil and garlic. Set aside. Drain the black olives and stuff with bits of anchovy. Place into marinade mixture. Cover and refrigerate overnight. Sprinkle with parsley before serving.

Taegu

Serves 6 — 8

Taegu* is a finger food to be enjoyed with cold beer.

1 (3-ounce) package	dried cuttlefish or cod,* shredded
1 teaspoon	toasted sesame seeds
1 teaspoon	paprika
$1/4$ teaspoon	chopped Hawaiian chili pepper*
$1/3$ cup	honey
$11/2$ teaspoons	sesame oil*
$1/4$ teaspoon	garlic juice
2 drops	red food coloring (optional)

Combine ingredients. Refrigerate in a jar for 3 days before serving.

Crab Mold

1 envelope	unflavored gelatin
4 teaspoons	cold water
1 (10³/4-ounce) can	cream of mushroom soup
6 ounces	cream cheese, softened
1/2	onion, grated
1 cup	finely chopped celery
1 cup	mayonnaise
6 ounces	crabmeat

Dissolve gelatin in cold water. In a saucepan, heat the soup and stir in gelatin. Add cream cheese and blend until smooth. Add onion, celery, mayonnaise and crabmeat. Mix well. Pour into a 5-cup mold. Chill for 3 hours until firm. Serve with bread, melba toast or crackers.

Sushi Bar

Sushi may be compared to a Danish open faced sandwich where one chooses from many toppings.

Basic Sushi Rice

3 cups	short grained rice
3¹/2 cups	water
3/4 – 1 cup	rice vinegar *
1/2 – ²/3 cup	sugar

In a heavy 3 to 4 quart pot, wash rice, stir and drain. Repeat this procedure until water is clear. Add water to rice. Cover and bring to a boil. Reduce heat and simmer for 20 minutes. Turn off heat and let rice stand for 15 minutes. Transfer to large bowl. Combine vinegar and sugar and pour over rice. Mix with a wooden paddle. Cover rice with a damp cloth until ready to serve.

continued...

Sushi Toppings

20 (8 x 8) sheets	sushi nori,* quartered
1/2 pound	shrimp, cooked, shelled and deveined
1/2 pound	crabmeat, cooked
1/2 pound	sashimi,* thinly sliced
1 (6 1/2-ounce) can	tuna, drained and mixed with 2 tablespoons soy sauce
1/2 cup	char siu,* thinly sliced
1 pound	kamaboko,* thinly sliced
1 1/2 pounds	steak, cooked and thinly sliced
1	avocado, peeled and thinly sliced
2	carrots, julienned and blanched
1/2 cup	daikon,* julienned
3 1/2 ounces	shiitake* mushrooms, soaked and thinly sliced
1 cup	pickled ginger*
1	cucumber, julienned
1/2 cup	chopped onion
1/4 cup	capers
24 (3-inch)	watercress tips, blanched
8 ounces	fresh mushrooms, sliced
2	egg omelet, thinly sliced
1 cup	mayonnaise
1/4 cup	ume boshi*
3/4 cup	soy sauce
4 tablespoons	wasabi* powder combined with 2 teaspoons water to make a paste
1	lemon, thinly sliced and quartered

Arrange the toppings on a tray, alternating colors and textures to create an interesting presentation.

To assemble, place a nori square in the palm of the left hand. Spread rice on nori. Place a dab of wasabi on rice. Choose a layer of toppings, place on rice and fold slightly with the right hand. Dip in soy sauce and eat.

Coconut Chips

Serves 4

1   fresh coconut, shelled and peeled

¹/₂ teaspoon   salt

Preheat oven to 325 degrees. Slice coconut meat into paper-thin chips 2 inches long. Spread a single layer of chips in a shallow baking pan and sprinkle with salt. Toast in oven for 30 minutes, stirring occasionally. Cool to room temperature. Store in a tightly covered jar.

Garlic Shrimp

Serves 10

3 – 5 pounds   medium to large shrimp, peeled and deveined

Marinade

1¹/₂ cups   mayonnaise

6 tablespoons   catsup

3 tablespoons   Worcestershire sauce

5 large cloves   garlic, crushed

3 tablespoons   capers, drained

1 tablespoon   dill weed

3 tablespoons   dill pickle juice

Cook shrimp in boiling salted water for 5 to 10 minutes. Rinse under cold water to stop the cooking process. Mix the marinade ingredients together. Marinate cooled shrimp in marinade. Cover and refrigerate for 24 hours. Stir every 12 hours.

Ono Seviche
Serves 4—6

Sweet Maui onions and fresh Island fish in a marinade that "cooks" the fish.

1 pound	Ono*
1 cup	fresh lemon juice
3 teaspoons	vegetable oil
1 (4-ounce) can	diced green chilies
4	tomatoes, peeled and cubed
1 small	Maui onion,* sliced
1 teaspoon	oregano
	salt and pepper to taste

Cut fish across the grain into bite-size pieces. Marinate in lemon juice for 4 hours. Refrigerate, stirring frequently. Drain lemon juice. Place fish in a serving bowl. Mix remaining ingredients together and add to the fish. Chill and serve with toothpicks.

Lime Shrimp
Serves 8

2 pounds	medium shrimp
3 cloves	garlic, minced
1/3 cup	olive oil
1/2 cup	fresh lime juice, reserve peels
1 ounce	dry vermouth
1 tablespoon	rock salt

In a large skillet, sauté shrimp and garlic in oil until shrimp turn pink. Turn off heat. Add lime juice and vermouth. Cover and steam for 3 minutes. Pour into a serving bowl. Sprinkle with rock salt and add quartered lime peels. Marinate for 1 hour. Note: Peel your own shrimp. Be sure to provide lots of napkins.

39

Pickled Shrimp

Serves 10 – 12

$1/2$ cup	celery tops
$3^1/2$ teaspoons	salt
$1/4$ cup	pickling spices
$2^1/2$ pounds	large shrimp
2 cups	sliced Maui onion*
7 – 8	bay leaves

Bring water to a boil with celery tops, salt and pickling spices. Add shrimp and cook until shrimp are pink. Drain shrimp. Cool, peel and devein. Layer shrimp and onions in a shallow dish. Add bay leaves.

Marinade

$1^1/4$ cups	vegetable oil
$3/4$ cup	white vinegar
$1^1/2$ teaspoons	salt
$2^1/2$ teaspoons	celery seed
$2^1/2$ teaspoons	capers with juice
dash	Tabasco

Combine ingredients, mix well and pour over shrimp. Cover and refrigerate for 24 hours. Serve with toothpicks.

Artichoke Balls

2 cloves	garlic, minced
2 tablespoons	olive oil
2 (8-ounce) cans	artichoke hearts, drained and chopped
2	eggs, slightly beaten
1/2 teaspoon	cayenne
1/2 cup	grated Parmesan cheese
1/2 cup	Italian-seasoned bread crumbs
1/4 cup	grated Parmesan cheese
1/4 cup	Italian-seasoned bread crumbs

Sauté garlic in oil but do not allow garlic to brown. Add artichokes, eggs and cayenne and cook over low heat for 5 minutes. Remove from heat and add Parmesan cheese and bread crumbs. Using 1 teaspoon of mixture, make into balls and roll in second mixture of cheese and bread crumbs. Chill and serve.

Poisson Cru

Serves 10 – 12

A traditional Tahitian way of preparing fish.

1 pound	fresh Ahi*
1/2 quart	lightly salted water
1 teaspoon	salt
1 cup	fresh lime juice
1 (12-ounce) can	coconut milk*
1 medium	tomato, coarsely chopped
1/2 medium	onion, coarsely chopped
1 medium	red bell pepper, thinly sliced
1/2 bunch	parsley, minced
	salt and pepper to taste
4 – 5 drops	Tabasco
	lettuce leaves
	Garnish: 2 hard cooked eggs, chopped

Cut fish across the grain into bite-size pieces. Soak fish in salted water for 15 minutes. Drain well. Sprinkle fish with salt and add lime juice. Soak for 10 minutes. Knead and mix well. Drain off 3/4 of the juice. Add coconut milk, tomato, onion, red pepper, parsley, salt, pepper and Tabasco. Marinate for 30 minutes. Serve on a bed of lettuce. Garnish with chopped egg. Serve with toothpicks.

Caviar
Hors D'oeuvre Ring

16 ounces	cream cheese, softened
1 bunch	parsley, chopped
1 teaspoon	lemon juice
1 (4-ounce) jar	red caviar
4	hard cooked eggs
3/4 cup	chopped green onions

Spread cream cheese 1/2 inch thick in a 10-inch quiche dish. Working from the outside in, make a ring of chopped parsley 1 inch wide. Sprinkle the parsley with lemon juice. Next, make a ring of red caviar. Follow with a ring of chopped egg white, then a ring of green onion and a center ring of chopped egg yolks. Serve chilled with crisp crackers or melba toast.

Florentine Dip

Makes 3 1/2 cups

1 (10-ounce) package	frozen chopped spinach
1 cup	mayonnaise
1 cup	sour cream
3/4 cup	chopped green onions
1/2 – 1 teaspoon	garlic salt
3/4 teaspoon	Beau Monde
1 teaspoon	Worcestershire sauce

Thaw spinach and drain well. In a bowl, combine spinach and remaining ingredients. Mix thoroughly. Cover and chill for 4 hours or overnight to blend flavors. Serve with assorted crudités.

Breadfruit Chips

The Island version of potato chips.

1 large	ripe solid breadfruit,* about 3 pounds
	vegetable oil
	salt

Peel breadfruit. Wash under running cold water and dry. Cut into four sections and remove the core. Slice as thinly as possible. An electric slicer works best. In a deep fat fryer, heat oil to 350 degrees and cook breadfruit until it is light golden yellow. Drain on paper towels and salt immediately. Store chips in an air-tight container. Chips may be frozen. Defrost at room tememprature for 30 minutes, then heat in a warm oven. Serve with Chutney Guacamole. Note: Breadfruit is ripe when white sap appears on the outside.

Chutney Guacamole

Makes 5 cups

The addition of chutney gives this extra zest!

4	ripe avocados, peeled and seeded
1/4 cup	chutney
2 cloves	garlic
2 – 3 small	limes, juiced
	salt, pepper and cayenne to taste
1 cup	chopped tomato

In a blender, place the meat of 3 avocados, the chutney, garlic and lime juice. Season to taste. Add the chopped tomato and remaining avocado. Blend for 10 seconds. Chill and serve.

Albert Schmid
Executive Chef
Dillingham Corporation
Honolulu, Hawaii

44

Standing Ovation Taco Dip

Serves 8 — 10

1 (10^1/2-ounce) can	jalapeño bean dip
8 ounces	jalapeño pepper dip
8 ounces	sour cream
1 (1.5-ounce) package	taco seasoning
1 small	onion, chopped
1 large	avocado, chopped
2 large	tomatoes, finely chopped
1 (4^1/4-ounce) can	sliced black olives
2 cups	shredded Cheddar cheese

On a serving platter, spread bean dip. For the next layer, spread pepper dip. Combine sour cream and taco seasoning and spread to form third layer. Top with onion, avocado, tomatoes and olives. Sprinkle cheese on top. Serve with tortilla chips.

Crudité Dip

Makes 2 cups

1 cup	mayonnaise
1 cup	sour cream
1 tablespoon	minced onion
1¼ tablespoons	minced parsley
½ teaspoon	garlic powder
1¼ tablespoons	dill weed
1¼ teaspoons	Beau Monde
½ teaspoon	curry powder
	assorted vegetables

Blend first eight ingredients together. Arrange raw fresh vegetables in alternating colors: cauliflower rosettes, radishes, celery sticks, carrot sticks, cucumber sticks, sliced red and green bell peppers, blanched fresh asparagus and mushroom caps.

Amanda's Dip

Makes 2 cups

12 ounces	cream cheese, softened
½ cup	Parmesan cheese
¼ cup	mayonnaise
½ teaspoon	oregano
¼ teaspoon	garlic powder

Combine ingredients and chill. Serve with celery sticks and cucumbers or with crackers.

Curry Dip

Makes 3 cups

*Carrots, celery, zucchini, cherry tomatoes, large black olives, cauli-
flower, mushrooms and broccoli make a colorful array of crudités
to serve with this dip.*

2 cups	mayonnaise
1/2 cup	sour cream
1/4 teaspoon	turmeric
2 tablespoons	curry powder
2 cloves	garlic, minced
4 teaspoons	sugar
1/2 – 1 teaspoon	salt
2 teaspoons	fresh lemon juice
1/4 cup	minced parsley

Combine ingredients. Blend thoroughly. Chill for 6 hours
or overnight to enhance flavor.

Curried Paté

Makes 3 cups

1 pound	liverwurst, softened
4 ounces	cream cheese, softened
1/3 cup	margarine, softened
1 tablespoon	curry powder
3 tablespoons	minced onion
3 tablespoons	minced parsley
3 tablespoons	brandy
	salt and pepper to taste

Combine liverwurst, cream cheese and margarine in
blender or food processor. Add remaining ingredients and blend
well. Chill. Serve with melba toast, mild crackers or Lavosh
(see index).

Hala-kahiki Paté   *Serves 10*

Hala-kahiki means pineapple and the finished paté is a semblance of this Island fruit.

1 pound	chicken livers
1 medium	onion, chopped
1 cup	butter
3/4 teaspoon	curry powder
	salt and pepper to taste
3 ounces	cream cheese
2 tablespoons	cognac or brandy

Garnish: 1 pineapple crown from a fresh whole pineapple and stuffed green olives, thinly sliced

Sauté liver and onion in 1/4 cup butter for 10 minutes. Season with curry powder, salt and pepper. Place liver mixture in blender or food processor with remaining butter, cream cheese and cognac. Blend until smooth. Chill until firm. To assemble, mold paté mixture into pineapple shape. Place pineapple crown at the top of the paté. Press olives onto paté to cover completely.

Single Hibiscus

Beverages

Blue Hawaii

Makes 1 drink

Blue Curaçao gives this drink its unique color.

2^1/2 ounces   pineapple juice
1 teaspoon   Orgeat syrup
1 ounce   Blue Curaçao
^{1}/2 ounce   vodka

Combine the ingredients. Fill a 12-ounce goblet with shaved ice and pour mixture over ice.

Al Hong
Trader Vic's Restaurant
Honolulu, Hawaii

Wicked Mai Tai Punch

Makes 2^1/2 to 3 quarts

38 ounces   dark Jamaican rum
7 ounces   Curaçao
5 ounces   Orgeat syrup
10 ounces   rock candy syrup
25 ounces   lemon juice
3 small   limes, juiced
3 – 4 cups   sugar
Garnish: Mint sprigs and pineapple spears

Mix the ingredients together. Serve over ice in a punch bowl or over crushed ice in a glass. Garnish with mint and pineapple spears.

Kimo's
Coconut Pipi

Makes 1 drink

A favorite from this waterfront restaurant in old Lahaina town.

1 cup	crushed ice
1 1/2 ounces	Kahlua
3 ounces	Half and Half or whipping cream
1 ounce	coconut syrup*
1 ounce	brandy

Garnish: Nutmeg

In a blender, pour Kahlua, cream, coconut syrup and brandy over crushed ice. Blend and serve in a 22-ounce snifter. Top with nutmeg.

Kimo's
Lahaina, Maui

Henry-Henrietta

Serves 1—2

A favorite sunset beverage served at the Outrigger Canoe Club at the foot of Diamond Head.

3 cups	crushed ice
2 ounces	orange juice or orange ade syrup
2 ounces	passion fruit* juice
2 ounces	vodka
1 ounce	grenadine

Put all ingredients in blender and blend 3 to 5 minutes until thick and icy. Serve in a 16-ounce glass for 1 serving or 2 8-ounce glasses for 2 servings. Note: For the Henrietta omit vodka.

Outrigger Canoe Club
Honolulu, Hawaii

53

White Sangria

Serves 6

4 cups	dry white wine
3/4 cup	Cointreau
1/2 cup	sugar
1 (10-ounce) bottle	club soda, chilled
1 small bunch	green grapes
1	sliced orange
1	sliced lemon
1	sliced lime

Garnish: Green apple wedges dipped in lemon juice

Mix white wine, Cointreau and sugar and chill. Just before serving, stir in the club soda, adding grapes, orange, lemon and lime slices. For each serving, garnish glass with an apple wedge.

Champagne Punch

Serves 16

1 fifth	champagne, chilled
3/4 cup	brandy
1/2 cup	Cointreau or Curaçao
2 cups	sparkling mineral water or soda, chilled

Garnish: Large fresh strawberries, sliced

Combine ingredients in a large punch bowl and float fresh strawberry slices on top. Ladle into punch cups or champagne glasses and garnish.

Kimo's Panini
Makes 1 drink

1 cup	crushed ice
3 medium	bananas
3 ounces	fresh orange juice
1$^1/_2$ ounces	light rum
1$^1/_2$ ounces	amber rum
dash	simple syrup*

Garnish: Mint leaf or orchid

Place ice in blender. Add bananas, juice, rums and syrup. Blend and serve in 22-ounce glass. Garnish with a mint leaf or an orchid.

Kimo's
Lahaina, Maui

Banana Cow
Makes 1 drink

3 ounces	milk
dash	vanilla
1$^1/_2$ teaspoons	sugar
1 medium	banana
1$^1/_2$ ounces	light rum
1 cup	crushed ice

Place ingredients in a blender. Blend and pour into a 12-ounce goblet.

Al Hong
Trader Vic's Restaurant
Honolulu, Hawaii

Bob Nob

A delicious holiday drink.

1 ounce	vodka
2 ounces	egg nog
$1/2$ ounce	Kahlua
	Garnish: Nutmeg

Stir vodka, egg nog and Kahlua together. Pour over ice cubes or crushed ice. Top with nutmeg.

Pink Palace

4 ounces	pineapple juice
$1/2$ ounce	lemon juice
1 ounce	Half and Half
$1^1/2$ ounces	cream of coconut
1 ounce	Grand Marnier
dash	Grenadine
	handful of ice
	Garnish: Pineapple, cherry and orchid

Combine ingredients and whirl in blender. Pour into a 22-ounce glass half filled with crushed ice. Garnish.

Royal Hawaiian Hotel
Honolulu, Hawaii

Buzz's Golden Coyne   *Serves 1*

1/4 ounce   white rum
1/4 ounce   Tuaca
1 ounce   milk
2 scoops   ice cream
Garnish: Whipped cream

Blend first three ingredients in a blender. Pour mixture into an 8-ounce tulip or wine glass. Top with scoops of ice cream and a dollop of whipped cream.

Bobby Lou Schneider
Buzz's Original Steak House-Moiliili
Honolulu, Hawaii

État Contente   *Serves 1*

Leaves you in a "contented state."

1 ounce   white crème de menthe
1 ounce   crème de cacao
4 ounces   strong coffee
Garnish: Whipped cream

Mix the white crème de menthe, crème de cacao and hot coffee. Serve in a small snifter or tulip wine glass. Garnish with whipped cream.

57

Volcano in Winter

Serves 4—6

$1/2$ gallon   vanilla ice cream
7 – 8 ounces   white creme de menthe
4 ounces   Triple Sec
Garnish: Nutmeg and chocolate shavings

Combine all ingredients in a blender. Whirl until smooth. Garnish and serve.

Hotel Hana Maui ChiChi

Serves 1

2 cups   crushed ice
$1^1/2$ ounces   vodka
6 ounces   pineapple juice
2 ounces   thick coconut syrup*

Blend in blender. For a frozen chichi, blend longer. Serve in a tall glass.

Hotel Hana Maui
Hana, Maui

Grandma Cooke's Iced Tea

Makes 3 quarts

Traditionally served in kamaaina homes.

3 quarts	water
6	tea bags
1^1/$_2$ – 2 cups	sugar
^{1}/$_2$ cup	water
1 bunch	fresh mint
	juice of 5 lemons

Bring water to a boil. Add tea bags and steep for 5 to 8 minutes. Remove bags. Boil sugar and half cup of water, stirring frequently. Add this syrup to the tea. Drop the mint into tea and let stand until cool. Stir in the lemon juice. Strain and chill. Serve over ice.

Hawaiian Punch

Serves 20

6 cups	orange juice
6 cups	guava* juice
6 cups	pineapple juice
1 quart	ginger ale
	Garnish: 1 thinly sliced orange

Mix juices together and chill. Just before serving, add ginger ale. Stir and garnish with floating orange slices. Note: For best flavor, use frozen guava juice.

Tropical Fruit Smoothie

Makes 1³/4 cups

1/2 papaya,* peeled and seeded

or

1 mango,* peeled and sliced
1 frozen banana, thickly sliced
1 tablespoon frozen passion fruit*
or orange juice concentrate
cold water

Put fruit in blender. Add water to nearly cover fruit. Blend until smooth. Serve immediately. Note: Ice cream may be added.

O.C.C. Iced Tea

Makes 1 gallon

1/2 gallon water
12 tea bags
3 sprigs fresh mint
1²/3 cups sugar
12 ounces pineapple juice
6 ounces lemon juice
Garnish: Mint sprigs and pineapple spears

Bring water to a boil and steep tea bags and mint. Remove mint after 3 minutes. Continue to steep tea until it is very dark. Remove tea bags. While tea is still warm, add sugar and juices, stirring to dissolve sugar. Pour into a gallon container, adding enough water to fill to the gallon level. Chill. Serve iced with mint sprigs and pineapple spears.

Oahu Country Club
Honolulu, Hawaii

Bird of Paradise

Salads and Salad Dressings

Royal Maile Salad

Serves 8

2 heads	Manoa lettuce,* cut in bite-size pieces
1/2 cup	chopped celery
1 cup	Bay shrimp, cooked
1	avocado, cut in half

Arrange lettuce on plates. Sprinkle with chopped celery and shrimp. Place two scoops of avocado on each serving. Top with dressing.

Celery Seed Dressing

1/2 cup	cider vinegar
1 tablespoon	Dijon mustard
1 teaspoon	celery seed
1/2 teaspoon	Worcestershire sauce
1	egg
3 teaspoons	sugar
1 1/2 teaspoons	salt
1/4 teaspoon	white pepper
1 clove	garlic, minced
1 teaspoon	sweet relish
1/2 teaspoon	Kitchen Bouquet
1/2 teaspoon	Maggi seasoning
	juice of 1/2 lemon
2 cups	vegetable oil

Combine vinegar, mustard, celery seed, Worcestershire, egg, sugar, salt, pepper, garlic, relish, Kitchen Bouquet, Maggi seasoning and lemon. Blend oil in slowly.

Maile Room
Kahala Hilton
Honolulu, Hawaii

Mandarin
Almond Salad

Serves 4—6

Excellent as a complement to a curry.

3 tablespoons	sugar
1/2 cup	slivered almonds
1 head	romaine lettuce, torn in bite-size pieces
1/2 head	iceberg lettuce, torn in bite-size pieces
1 cup	chopped green onions
3/4 cup	chopped celery
1 (11-ounce) can	mandarin oranges, drained

Dressing

2 tablespoons	cider vinegar
1/4 cup	vegetable oil
2 tablespoons	chopped fresh parsley
1/2 teaspoon	salt
dash	Tabasco
1 tablespoon	brown sugar (optional)

In a saucepan over medium heat, melt the sugar until pale caramel in color. Add almonds and stir to coat. Remove from heat and pour on foil to cool. Chop when cooled. Set aside. In a large salad bowl, combine the lettuce leaves, onions and celery. Refrigerate two hours or overnight to enhance flavor. In a small bowl, mix the dressing ingredients and refrigerate. When ready to serve, add the almonds, oranges and dressing to the lettuce and toss.

The Bistro's Caesar Salad

Serves 2

A favorite from the Bistro at Diamond Head.

1/2 teaspoon	salt
1 clove	garlic
	juice of 1/2 lemon
2 tablespoons	wine vinegar
1 teaspoon	Dijon mustard
1/3 teaspoon	anchovy paste
1	coddled egg
1/4 teaspoon	freshly ground black pepper
3 teaspoons	Worcestershire sauce
3 – 4 tablespoons	olive oil
1 head	romaine lettuce, torn in bite-size pieces
1/4 cup	shredded Parmesan cheese
	croutons (see index)

"First take the wooden bowl, sprinkle salt in the bottom. Impale garlic clove on fork and rub (gently) around (the garlic clove, that is!). Take half a lemon and squeeze into bowl. Now, remove lemon pips and any garlic that may be left in bowl. Sprinkle wine vinegar to augment juice of lemon; more vinegar for a dry lemon, less for a juicy one. Place a teaspoon of mustard (make it a good one), a third teaspoon of anchovy paste (be careful, this stuff is very salty). At this point, take the egg that should be in the hot water (and if it's not, you're going to be) and break it into the bowl. Grind 15 to 20 turns of pepper over yolk of egg. (This will enable you to see how much pepper is coming out of the grinder). Turn a bottle of Worcestershire sauce upside down and encircle bowl three times (approximately 3 teaspoons). While mixing this entire mess, smile and add three or four tablespoons (wooden mixing spoon) full of olive oil. Mix well. Add romaine lettuce and 2 generous spoons of Parmesan cheese. Toss. Put on salad plates. Sprinkle with croutons. Serve."

Spinach Salad with Chutney Dressing

Serves 2—4

1 pound   fresh spinach, trimmed and torn in bite-size pieces

6   fresh mushrooms, sliced

1 cup   water chestnuts,* sliced

6 slices   bacon, fried and crumbled

1/3 – 1/2 cup   shredded Gruyère cheese

Dressing

1/4 cup   wine vinegar

1 clove   garlic, minced

2 – 3 tablespoons   chutney

2 teaspoons   sugar

2 tablespoons   coarsely ground Dijon mustard

1/3 – 1/2 cup   vegetable oil

salt and freshly ground black pepper to taste

In a blender, combine dressing ingredients except the oil. Blend until smooth. Add the oil, blend and adjust seasonings. Refrigerate. Bring dressing to room temperature before serving. Combine salad ingredients. Pour dressing over salad, toss and serve.

Basic Spinach Salad *Serves 4—6*

2 bunches spinach, washed, trimmed, and torn in
        bite-size pieces
1/2 pound bacon, fried and crumbled
2 hard-cooked eggs, chopped
1 cup sliced fresh mushrooms

Dressing

1 egg
1 tablespoon finely grated Parmesan cheese
2 tablespoons Dijon mustard
3 tablespoons lemon juice
1 teaspoon Worcestershire sauce
1 tablespoon sugar
1/2 teaspoon salt
dash white pepper
1/4 cup vegetable oil

    Prepare salad ingredients. Blend the dressing ingredients except the oil. Add oil and beat thoroughly. Store in the refrigerator if not used immediately. Combine spinach, bacon, egg and mushrooms. Add dressing and toss lightly.

Layered Spinach Salad

Serves 8 – 10

This salad is assembled the night before to allow the flavors to mingle. It makes an impressive presentation when served in a clear glass bowl.

2 bunches	spinach, washed, trimmed and torn in bite-size pieces
1 teaspoon	sugar
6	hard-cooked eggs, chopped
1/2 pound	ham, julienned
1 (10-ounce) box	frozen petite peas, half thawed
1	Maui onion,* thinly sliced and separated in rings
1 cup	sour cream
1 cup	mayonnaise
1/2 pound	Swiss cheese, grated
1 pound	bacon, fried and crumbled

On the bottom of a 4-quart shallow glass serving bowl, place 1/2 of the spinach. Sprinkle with 1/2 teaspoon sugar. Next layer the eggs and ham followed by another layer of spinach and 1/2 teaspoon sugar. Add the peas and the onion. Mix the sour cream and mayonnaise and spread evenly to the edge of the salad to seal. Cover and refrigerate over night. When ready to serve, top with the grated Swiss cheese and crumbled bacon.

Korean Spinach Salad   *Serves 4*

1 pound	fresh spinach, washed and trimmed
1 tablespoon	soy sauce
1 1/2 tablespoons	sesame oil*
1 tablespoon	sesame seeds
1 clove	garlic, minced
1 teaspoon	sugar
1 teaspoon	cider vinegar
	pepper to taste

Steam the spinach in the moisture that clings to its leaves until tender, about 3 minutes. Drain and squeeze out as much water as possible. Chop coarsely. Combine remaining ingredients and mix with spinach. Serve hot or cold.

Cauliflower Shrimp Salad   *Serves 6—8*

1 medium	cauliflower, shredded or finely chopped
2 pounds	small shrimp, cooked and deveined
1/2 cup	ripe pitted olives
1 cup	mayonnaise
1 1/2 tablespoons	Dijon mustard
1/4 cup	sour cream
	Boston or Manoa* lettuce leaves
	paprika

Combine cauliflower, shrimp and olives. Mix mayonnaise with mustard and sour cream. Toss salad with dressing. Arrange in bowl lined with lettuce leaves. Sprinkle with paprika.

70

Peas and Peanut Slaw *Serves 4—6*

1 (10-ounce) package frozen peas
2 cups finely shredded cabbage
1 green onion, thinly sliced

Dressing

1/4 cup sour cream
1/4 cup mayonnaise
1 teaspoon prepared mustard
1 teaspoon white wine vinegar
1/4 teaspoon curry powder
1/4 teaspoon salt
dash pepper
*Garnish: 3/4 cup salted Spanish
peanuts*

Turn frozen peas into a colander and rinse until thawed.
Drain. Combine peas, cabbage and onion. Mix dressing ingredients and pour over salad, mixing lightly. Cover and chill, preferably overnight. Garnish and serve.

Coleslaw *Serves 4—6*

1 cup whipping cream, whipped
1/2 cup sugar
1/2 cup cider vinegar
1 head cabbage, finely shredded

Add sugar and vinegar to the whipped cream. Fold in
cabbage. Refrigerate for 2 hours.

71

Mexican Salad

Serves 6

1 pound	lean ground beef
1 large	onion, chopped
1 (16-ounce) can	red kidney beans, rinsed and drained
1$^{1}/_{2}$ teaspoons	cumin seeds
$^{1}/_{2}$ teaspoon	chili powder
$^{1}/_{2}$ teaspoon	garlic salt
1 head	iceberg lettuce, torn in bite-size pieces
2	tomatoes, chopped
1	avocado, diced
3	green onions, chopped
1 (3-ounce) can	sliced olives
1 (2-ounce) jar	chopped pimiento
2 cups	shredded Cheddar cheese
1 (8-ounce) bag	tortilla chips, crushed
1 cup	Green Goddess salad dressing (see index) or your own favorite dressing
	salt and pepper to taste
	hot taco sauce (optional)

In a skillet, sauté beef and onions until onion is transparent. Drain. Add beans and spices and simmer for 10 minutes. In a large serving bowl, combine lettuce, tomatoes, avocado, onions, olives and pimiento and top with cheese. Add warm beef mixture, chips and dressing. Toss. Season. Note: For a spicier salad, top individual portions with hot taco sauce or Salsa Cocina (see index).

Chinese Salad   *Serves 4—6*

Dressing should be made a day in advance.

1 (5-ounce) can	Chow Mein noodles
3 tablespoons	melted butter
1 teaspoon	curry powder
2 teaspoons	Worcestershire sauce
1/2 teaspoon	freshly ground pepper
1 head	romaine lettuce, torn in bite-size pieces
1/2 head	iceberg lettuce, torn in bite-size pieces
1/3 cup	sliced ripe olives

Dressing

1 cup	olive oil
1 cup	red wine vinegar
1 clove	garlic, minced
1/2 teaspoon	salt
1/4 teaspoon	pepper
1 tablespoon	sugar

Combine the dressing ingredients in a jar. Shake and let stand 24 hours. Preheat oven to 200 degrees. In a shallow pan, mix noodles with butter and seasonings. Bake for 15 minutes, stirring occasionally. Place greens and olives in a salad bowl. Add noodles while still warm and toss with dressing.

Green Papaya Salad

Serves 2–4

1 clove	garlic
1 – 3	Hawaiian chili peppers*
1/2 pound	green papaya,* peeled, seeded and shredded
1	tomato, sliced
2 tablespoons	Thai fish sauce*
3 tablespoons	lime juice
1 head	lettuce or cabbage, shredded

Grind garlic with chili peppers. Combine shredded papaya, sliced tomato, fish sauce, lime juice and pepper-garlic mixture and mix well. Serve with lettuce or cabbage.

Keo Sananikone
Keo's
Honolulu, Hawaii

Bean Sprout Namul

Serves 4

12 ounces	bean sprouts
2 tablespoons	soy sauce
2 teaspoons	sesame oil*
1 tablespoon	rice vinegar*
1/4 – 1/2 cup	chopped green onion
1 tablespoon	sesame seeds

In a saucepan, bring 2 cups of water to a boil and boil bean sprouts for 1 to 2 minutes. Rinse in cold water and drain. Combine the remaining ingredients and mix with sprouts. Cover and chill 1 hour.

Somen Noodle Salad   *Serves 10*

This colorful salad is an excellent buffet or picnic dish.

2 (9-ounce) packages	somen noodles,* boiled and rinsed with cold water
1/2 head	iceberg lettuce, shredded
1/2 pound	char siu* or ham, sliced into strips
2	egg omelet, julienned
1	cucumber, sliced into strips
1 package	kamaboko,* sliced into strips
1 (7-ounce) can	crabmeat, shredded (optional)
4	green onions, finely chopped
2 cups	fresh watercress, cut in 2-inch pieces

Dressing

1/3 cup	rice vinegar*
1 tablespoon	vegetable oil
1 tablespoon	sesame oil*
1/2 cup	soy sauce
1/4 cup	sugar
2 tablespoons	sesame seeds

Garnish: Chinese parsley and sliced water chestnuts**

Toss the salad with dressing and serve.

Chinese Chicken Salad   *Serves 10*

10	boneless chicken breasts, skinned
2 cups	julienned ham
1	cucumber, peeled, seeded and julienned
1/3 cup	chopped peanuts
2	green onions, thinly sliced
1 small head	iceberg lettuce, shredded

Dressing

4 tablespoons	peanut butter
3 tablespoons	soy sauce
1 tablespoon	dry mustard
3 tablespoons	cider vinegar
1/2 teaspoon	salt
1 teaspoon	toasted sesame seeds
3 cloves	garlic, minced
1/4 teaspoon	white pepper
1/4 teaspoon	crushed red pepper

Simmer chicken breasts in water until tender. Cool. Shred by hand to make approximately 5 cups. Mix dressing ingredients in a bowl. Pour over chicken and ham. Mix until well coated. Add cucumber, peanuts and green onion. Toss. Place lettuce on individual plates and divide chicken salad equally.

Dana's Tofu Salad

Serves 6—8

A unique combination: Tuna and tofu are combined in a salad with a spicy oriental dressing.

18-ounces	firm tofu,* drained, cubed in 1-inch pieces
1 (8-ounce) can	tuna, drained and flaked
1 small	Maui onion,* finely chopped
1 small	cucumber, thinly sliced
1 small	tomato, thinly sliced

Dressing

2/3 cup	peanut oil
1 clove	garlic, minced
1/2 teaspoon	sesame oil*
1 tablespoon	toasted sesame seeds
2/3 cup	soy sauce
dash	Tabasco

Garnish: 3 green onions, chopped

Gently mix tofu, tuna, onion, cucumber and tomato. Chill until ready to serve. To prepare dressing, sauté garlic in oil in a saucepan until garlic turns brown. Cool and add sesame oil, sesame seeds, soy sauce and Tabasco. Pour dressing over salad, garnish and serve.

Namasu with Carrots   *Serves 6—8*

A Japanese salad or pupu made from pickled cucumbers.

2	cucumbers, unpeeled
1	carrot, peeled
2 tablespoons	Hawaiian rock salt*
1 (2¹/2-ounce) package	long rice*
²/3 cup	brown sugar
1 cup	rice vinegar*

Slice cucumbers and carrots in ¹/4-inch slices and spread them in a flat container. Sprinkle the slices with rock salt. Let stand 1 hour and lightly squeeze out the liquid from the cucumbers. Meanwhile, cover long rice with water and soak in a saucepan for 15 minutes. Boil the water and long rice for 5 minutes, then drain and cut rice in 2-inch lengths. In another saucepan, mix the brown sugar and vinegar. Heat and stir until sugar dissolves. Blend all ingredients and refrigerate, covered, for up to 5 days or until ready to serve. Note: Ginger slivers* and/or canned abalone slivers may be added at the last minute.

Papaya Salad

1 small	Maui onion,* thinly sliced
1	semi-ripe papaya,* peeled, seeded and cubed
1 bunch	watercress, trimmed and cut in 1-inch pieces
	lettuce leaves

Dressing

1/3 cup	tarragon vinegar
1 tablespoon	honey
1 tablespoon	poppy seeds
1 tablespoon	chopped fresh mint
1/2 teaspoon	ground coriander
dash	white pepper

Soak onion in a bowl of water for 10 minutes. Drain. Add papaya and refrigerate for 1 hour. Combine dressing ingredients. Toss papaya, onion and watercress with dressing. Serve on bed of lettuce.

Kim Chee Salad

1 head	cabbage, cut in bite-size pieces
1/4 cup	coarse salt
1 small	carrot, julienned
4	green onions, sliced
5 cloves	garlic, minced
1/2 cup	cider vinegar
1 1/2 teaspoons	cayenne or crushed red pepper
2 teaspoons	sesame oil*
2 teaspoons	toasted sesame seeds
4 tablespoons	vegetable oil
3 teaspoons	sugar

Sprinkle salt over cabbage, toss and set aside for 20 minutes. Rinse and drain cabbage in salad dryer. In large bowl, combine cabbage with vegetables and seasonings. Toss well. Refrigerate and toss at intervals to blend flavors. Note: The longer this sits, the better the flavor.

Russian Raspberry Cream Mold

Serves 6—8

1 (3-ounce) package raspberry or strawberry Jello
1 cup boiling water
1 tablespoon lemon juice
1 (10-ounce) package frozen raspberries or strawberries, thawed

Cream layer

1 envelope unflavored gelatin
1/2 cup warm water
1 cup Half and Half
1/2 cup sugar
1 cup sour cream
1 teaspoon vanilla

Dissolve Jello in water. Add lemon juice and fruit. Pour into a 6-cup mold and refrigerate until firm. In a mixing bowl, soften the gelatin in warm water and set aside. In a saucepan, heat the Half and Half and sugar over low heat until the sugar dissolves. Do not boil. Add cream mixture to gelatin. Add sour cream and vanilla and beat until smooth. Pour over chilled Jello layer slowly. Refrigerate until firm.

Cranberry Salad with Pineapple

Serves 8

4 cups	fresh cranberries
2	oranges
2 cups	sugar
1 cup	seeded grapes, red or green
1 (15¼-ounce) can	pineapple chunks
1 cup	small marshmallows
1 cup	whipping cream, whipped to peaks
	Garnish: Chopped nuts

Put cranberries, juice from both oranges and peel from one through meat grinder or food processor. Add sugar and let stand for 12 hours, stirring occasionally. Drain. Add grapes, pineapple and marshmallows. Fold in whipped cream. Garnish and serve.

Surprise Salad

Serves 8

The Jello in this salad is mixed "dry." Enjoy a little kitchen chemistry.

1 (16-ounce) carton	small curd cottage cheese, drained
1 (3-ounce) package	orange Jello
1 (15¼-ounce) can	crushed pineapple, drained
1 (11-ounce) can	mandarin oranges, drained
1 (4-ounce) carton	whipped topping, thawed

In a large mixing bowl, combine cottage cheese and dry Jello and mix thoroughly. Fold in fruits and whipped topping. Chill 1 hour or overnight.

Red Hot Salad   *Serves 12*

A different idea for Jello.

3 (3-ounce) packages	raspberry Jello
1¼ cups	boiling water
3 (1-pound) cans	stewed tomatoes, chopped
6 drops	Tabasco
	lettuce leaves

Dressing

1 pint	sour cream
1 tablespoon	horseradish
¹/₂ teaspoon	salt
¹/₂ teaspoon	sugar

Dissolve Jello in water. Stir in tomatoes and Tabasco and pour into a 12-cup mold. Chill until firm. Combine dressing ingredients and refrigerate. Unmold salad on a bed of lettuce and serve with dressing.

Bacon Dressing   *Serves 4*

4 slices	bacon, fried and crumbled, reserve drippings
3 tablespoons	white wine vinegar
2 tablespoons	sugar
1	egg, beaten
	salt and pepper to taste

Cool bacon drippings slightly and add vinegar, sugar and egg. Whisk vigorously until thickened. Add bacon and stir. Season and serve over lettuce, spinach or vegetable salad.

Herb Dressing
Makes 1 1/2 cups

1 teaspoon	oregano
1 1/2 teaspoons	salt
1 teaspoon	pepper
1 teaspoon	dill weed
1/2 cup	parsley
2 tablespoons	Dijon mustard
2 tablespoons	sugar
3 cloves	garlic
1/4 cup	cider or wine vinegar
3/4 cup	vegetable oil

Place ingredients in a food processor and blend well.

Lisa's French Dressing
Makes 2 cups

1 teaspoon	salt
1/2 teaspoon	dry mustard
1/4 teaspoon	paprika
1 teaspoon	celery seed
4 tablespoons	sugar
1/4 teaspoon	black pepper
1 teaspoon	basil
1 bunch	parsley, stems removed
3 large cloves	garlic
1/4 cup	catsup
1/2 cup	vinegar
3/4 cup	olive oil

Blend ingredients in a food processor and refrigerate.

Sauce Vinaigrette

Makes 5 cups

2 cups	red wine vinegar
2 cups	olive oil
2 tablespoons	dry mustard
1 tablespoon	salt
1 tablespoon	white pepper
4 cloves	garlic, crushed
1/2 cup	finely chopped parsley
1/2 cup	finely chopped onion
1/4 cup	finely chopped capers
1/4 cup	finely chopped dill pickles
2 large	tomatoes, peeled, seeded and chopped
3	hard-cooked eggs, chopped

Combine first six ingredients and chill for 24 hours. Add remaining ingredients and serve with tossed greens, sliced avocado, asparagus spears or lightly cooked vegetables.

Albert Schmid
Executive Chef
Dillingham Corporation
Honolulu, Hawaii

Tarragon Dressing

Makes 2/3 cup

1/4 cup	chopped parsley
1 clove	garlic, minced
1 teaspoon	sugar
1/4 cup	vegetable oil
2 tablespoons	cider vinegar
1 teaspoon	tarragon
2 teaspoons	Dijon mustard
1 teaspoon	salt
1/4 teaspoon	pepper

Blend ingredients and refrigerate 3 to 4 hours.

Dijon Dressing

Makes 3/4 cup

1 tablespoon	Dijon mustard
1	egg yolk
1 clove	garlic, minced
1 tablespoon	red wine vinegar
2 tablespoons	dry vermouth
dash	Tabasco
1/3 cup	peanut oil
	salt and freshly ground pepper to taste

Place mustard, egg yolk and garlic in a mixing bowl. With wire whisk, beat in vinegar, vermouth and Tabasco. Add oil, beating vigorously. Season. Note: Serve with one bunch of watercress, thinly sliced endive and sliced mushrooms.

Creamy Louis Dressing

Makes 2¹/2 cups

Excellent on crab, shrimp, chicken or tuna salad.

1 cup	mayonnaise
¹/3 cup	chili sauce
3 tablespoons	pickle relish
3 tablespoons	finely chopped green pepper
2 tablespoons	finely chopped celery
¹/4 teaspoon	paprika
¹/4 – ¹/2 teaspoon	salt
dash	Tabasco
¹/2 cup	whipping cream, whipped

Combine all ingredients except cream. Blend well. Fold in whipped cream. Cover and chill until ready to serve. Store for up to 4 days.

Tofu Dressing

Makes 4 cups

12 ounces	soft tofu,* drained
4 tablespoons	vegetable oil
3 tablespoons	lemon juice
2 cloves	garlic, minced
¹/2 – 1 teaspoon	salt
dash	white pepper
1 tablespoon	freshly grated Parmesan or Romano cheese

In a food processor or blender, process tofu, slowly adding oil and lemon juice. Add garlic, seasonings and cheese. Blend and chill.

Tiare's Salad Dressing

Makes 2¹/₂ cups

1 small	onion, chopped
1 cup	mayonnaise
¹/₃ cup	vegetable oil
¹/₄ cup	catsup
2 tablespoons	sugar
2 tablespoons	wine vinegar
1 teaspoon	dry mustard
¹/₂ teaspoon	salt
¹/₂ teaspoon	paprika
¹/₄ teaspoon	celery seed
dash	pepper
4 ounces	crumbled bleu cheese

Put all ingredients except cheese in a blender and whirl until smooth. Remove from blender and stir in bleu cheese. Cover, chill and serve over tossed salad.

Maharajah Dressing

Makes 1 cup

An excellent dressing for seafood or chicken salad.

1 cup	mayonnaise
1 tablespoon	lemon juice
1¹/₂ tablespoons	curry powder
¹/₂ teaspoon	Worcestershire sauce
3 drops	Tabasco
	salt and white pepper to taste

Combine ingredients and chill. Note: Also good as a dip for fresh vegetables.

Waioli Guava Dressing

Makes 3 cups

1 cup	mayonnaise
1 cup	catsup
1/4 cup	vinegar
1/2 cup	vegetable oil
1 teaspoon	dry mustard
2 teaspoons	lemon juice
1/2 cup	guava* jelly or jam
1/2 teaspoon	garlic salt

Combine ingredients and beat until well blended. Chill.

Waioli Tea Room
Honolulu, Hawaii

Ginger Salad Dressing

Makes 1 1/2 cups

2-inch piece	fresh ginger,* peeled
3 cloves	garlic
1/2 cup	parsley
2 tablespoons	Dijon mustard
2 tablespoons	honey
1 1/2 teaspoons	salt
1/2 teaspoon	pepper
1/4 cup	cider or wine vinegar
3/4 cup	vegetable oil

In a food processor, mince the fresh ginger and garlic. Add remaining ingredients and blend well.

Green Goddess
Salad Dressing

Makes 1¹/2 cups

2 teaspoons	tarragon vinegar
3 tablespoons	chopped parsley
3 tablespoons	chopped green onion
2 teaspoons	anchovy fillets
2 teaspoons	chives
1 teaspoon	capers
1 clove	garlic
1/8 teaspoon	salt
1 cup	mayonnaise

Combine ingredients except mayonnaise in a food processor. Process. Add mayonnaise and process thoroughly. Chill for two hours.

Ruby French
Dressing

Makes 2 cups

Equally delicious on fresh fruit or tossed green salad.

1/2 cup	sugar
1/4 cup	lemon juice
1/2 cup	catsup
1 cup	vegetable oil
2 tablespoons	cider vinegar
1/2 teaspoon	salt
2 tablespoons	chopped onion
2 teaspoons	celery seed

Combine all ingredients in blender. Mix well and refrigerate.

Papaya Seed Dressing   *Makes 1 cup*

Excellent on your favorite fruit or green salad.

1/4 cup	tarragon vinegar
1/4 cup	sugar
1/4 teaspoon	salt
1/2 teaspoon	dry mustard
1/2 cup	vegetable oil
1/2 small	onion, finely chopped
1 tablespoon	fresh papaya* seeds

Put vinegar and dry ingredients in a blender. With motor running, add oil in a steady stream and add onion. Add papaya seeds and blend only until the seeds resemble coarsely ground pepper. Chill for 1 hour before serving.

Pineapple Lemon Mint Dressing   *Makes 1 1/2 cups*

2/3 cup	vegetable oil
1/3 cup	unsweetened pineapple juice
1 teaspoon	grated lemon peel
2 tablespoons	lemon juice
1 – 2 teaspoons	chopped fresh mint
3/4 teaspoon	salt
1/2 teaspoon	dry mustard

Combine ingredients in a jar and shake vigorously until blended. Refrigerate. Serve over fruit or green salad.

Poppy Seed Dressing

Makes 3 – 3¹/2 cups

1¹/₃ cups	sugar
2 teaspoons	salt
2 teaspoons	dry mustard
²/₃ cup	white vinegar
3 tablespoons	Maui onion,* finely chopped
2 cups	vegetable oil
3 tablespoons	poppy seeds

Combine sugar, salt, dry mustard and vinegar. Add onion and mix well. Pour into a blender and slowly add oil, blending until thick. Stir in the poppy seeds. Store in the refrigerator. Note: This keeps well for 3 to 4 weeks. If it separates, shake well or beat. Serve with fresh fruit salads.

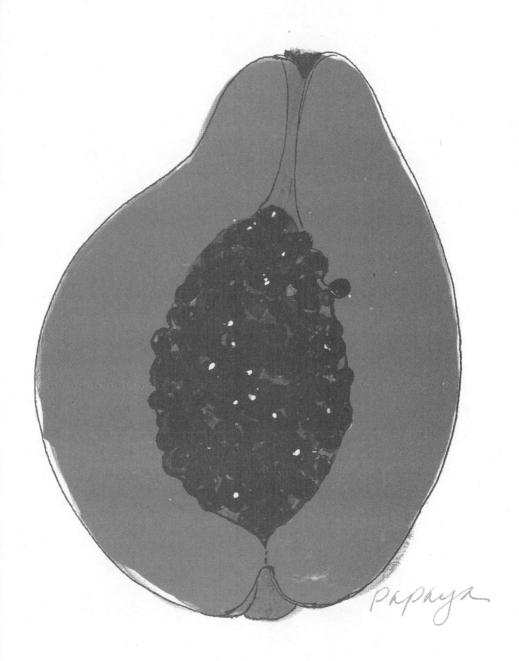

papaya

Soups

Cold Cream of Artichoke Soup

Serves 14

2 large	onions, chopped
2 tablespoons	butter
4 (14^1/2-ounce) cans	artichoke hearts, drained and chopped
6 cups	chicken stock or enhanced broth (see note)
1 teaspoon	salt
1 teaspoon	thyme
^{1}/2 teaspoon	oregano
1 teaspoon	pepper
2 tablespoons	fresh lemon juice
1 teaspoon	chicken stock base
^{1}/2 teaspoon	Tabasco
2 cups	Half and Half
2 cups	whipping cream

Garnish: Chopped parsley or chives

In a heavy saucepan, sauté onions in butter until soft. Add artichoke hearts and simmer for 5 minutes. Add stock, salt, thyme, oregano and pepper. Cover and simmer for 15 minutes. Cool and purée in blender or food processor. Strain. Add lemon juice, chicken stock base, Tabasco, Half and Half and whipping cream. Store in a covered container. Refrigerate for 3 hours or overnight. Garnish and serve. Note: Enhance canned chicken broth by simmering it for 45 minutes with 2 sliced carrots, 2 celery stalks, and 1 sliced onion. Remove vegetables.

Paul Koy's
Yokohama Soup Glacée *Serves 8*

This recipe is from Paul Koy, long-time chef at the Royal Hawaiian Hotel on Waikiki Beach.

$1/4$ pound	butter
2 tablespoons	finely chopped shallots
$1^1/2$ cups	dry white wine
$1/2$ cup	flour
3 cups	clam juice
3 cups	beef broth
$2^1/2$ cups	whipping cream
$1/4$ teaspoon	salt
$1/2$ cup	cooked purée of konbu *
	or fresh spinach

Garnish: $1/2$ cup whipped cream and grated Parmesan cheese

In a deep saucepan, sauté shallots for 2 minutes, making sure shallots do not brown. Add wine and reduce to half of its quantity. Stir in flour with a whisk until mixture is smooth. Combine clam juice and beef broth and boil. Heat cream. Add liquids individually to flour mixture, stirring each addition until smooth. Season with salt. Add seaweed or spinach and simmer for 15 to 20 minutes. Fill soup cups 3/4 full. Top each cup with a heaping teaspoonful of whipped cream. Sprinkle Parmesan cheese on top. Place under broiler until top of soup reaches a golden brown color. Serve with cheese straws or crackers.

Mahimahi Chowder

Serves 10—12

6 slices	bacon, cut into small pieces
2 medium	onions, chopped
3 stalks	celery, chopped
8 sprigs	parsley, chopped
2	potatoes, peeled and diced
1/2 cup	water
12 ounces	mahimahi* fillets
1/4 teaspoon	white pepper
1 1/2 – 2 teaspoons	garlic salt
2 cups	whipping cream
2 1/2 cups	Half and Half
3/4 – 1 tablespoon	cornstarch
1/2 ounce	dry sherry

Garnish: Chopped parsley

Fry bacon in a heavy saucepan. Remove bacon, using drippings to sauté onion, celery and parsley until tender. Add diced potatoes and water to saucepan. Cover and simmer until potatoes are tender. Stir in bacon. Place fillets on top of soup, cover and steam until fish flakes easily. Break into bite-size pieces and stir into soup. Add white pepper and garlic salt. Stir in cream and Half and Half and heat thoroughly. In a separate cup, combine cornstarch and sherry. Slowly stir into chowder to thicken. Heat just to boiling, remove from heat and serve immediately. Garnish with parsley.

Portuguese Bean Soup   *Serves 10*

An Island favorite.

1/2 pound	dried kidney beans
2 – 3	ham hocks
1 1/2 – 2 pounds	hot Portuguese sausage,* cut in 1/2-inch slices, sautéed and drained
1 (8-ounce) can	tomato sauce
2 large	baking potatoes, cut into 3/4-inch cubes
1	onion, sliced
3	carrots, sliced
3 stalks	celery, sliced
3 tablespoons	minced parsley
1 clove	garlic, minced
1 tablespoon	lemon juice
1/2 head	medium cabbage, shredded (optional)
1/2 cup	uncooked macaroni (optional)
1 bunch	watercress, chopped (optional)
	salt, pepper and allspice to taste

Cover beans with water and soak overnight. Drain. Cover ham hocks with water and cook for 1 to 1 1/2 hours. Remove ham hocks, shred meat and discard bone and fat. Add beans to liquid and cook for 1 hour. Return meat to soup along with Portuguese sausage. Cook for 10 minutes. Add tomato sauce, potatoes, onion, carrots, celery, parsley, garlic and lemon juice. Simmer until vegetables are tender. Add cabbage, macaroni, watercress, salt, pepper and allspice. Simmer for 10 minutes or until macaroni is tender.

Portuguese Soup

Serves 8

An easier version.

1/4 pound	bacon, diced
1	onion, chopped
1/4 pound	hot Portuguese sausage,* sliced
1 (8-ounce) can	tomatoes, chopped
1 (17-ounce) can	kidney beans
4 cups	beef broth
1 cup	shredded cabbage
	salt and pepper to taste

In a large soup pot, fry the bacon and onion together until slightly brown. Add the sausage, tomatoes, kidney beans and beef broth. Simmer until tender, frequently skimming off the fat. Add cabbage and simmer until cabbage is soft. Season. Serve hot.

Albert Schmid
Executive Chef
Dillingham Corporation
Honolulu, Hawaii

Snow Pea Soup

Serves 4 – 6

4 tablespoons	butter
1 small clove	garlic, minced
1 medium	red onion, chopped
$^1/_3$ cup	flour
3 cups	chicken stock or broth, boiling
1 pound	fresh snow peas,* strings removed
1 cup	milk
2 – 2$^1/_2$ teaspoons	grated fresh ginger*
	salt and white pepper to taste

In a large, heavy saucepan, sauté the garlic and onion in butter until soft and translucent, about 5 minutes. Remove saucepan from heat. Add flour and stir until well blended. Add chicken stock and mix thoroughly. Return to medium heat and cook until thickened and smooth. Add the snow peas and cook for 5 minutes until snow peas are puffed and bright green but not too soft. Add the milk and cook for an additional 3 minutes. Purée soup mixture in a blender or food processor until very smooth. Reheat for 5 minutes. Add ginger, salt and white pepper to taste. Serve hot. Note: The puréeing step is optional.

Curried Zucchini Soup *Serves 8*

4 tablespoons	butter
2 pounds	zucchini, unpeeled and thinly sliced
4 tablespoons	finely chopped shallots
2 teaspoons	curry powder
1 teaspoon	salt
1 cup	chicken broth
2 cups	Half and Half

Garnish: Sour cream and chives

Melt butter in a skillet and add zucchini and shallots. Cover and simmer for 10 minutes. Do not brown. Add curry powder and salt and continue to cook until tender. Cool. Put zucchini in a food processor and process until smooth. Add chicken broth and Half and Half. Process until mixture is creamy. Chill. Garnish.

Tad and Pat, Ltd.
Honolulu, Hawaii

Miso Soup

1 teaspoon	sesame oil*
1 tablespoon	vegetable oil
1	red onion, finely chopped
1½ teaspoons	flour
4 cups	chicken broth
4 tablespoons	light or dark miso*
¼ cup	mirin*
2	carrots, peeled and thinly sliced diagonally
¼ cup	chopped parsley
3 tablespoons	soy sauce
	Garnish: Green onion, diagonally sliced

In a heavy saucepan, sauté the onion in oils until soft. Stir in flour. Add broth. Stir with a whisk to remove any lumps. Continue stirring while adding miso. Simmer for 5 minutes. Add mirin and stir constantly. Add carrots and simmer for 5 to 10 minutes. Add parsley and soy sauce. Garnish and serve.

Miso Soup from the P.K.   *Serves 10*

      7 cups   water
1 handful   hana katsuo*
   5 ounces   aka miso*
   4 ounces   shiro miso*

*Garnish: Chopped green onion and cubed tofu**

Bring water to a boil and turn off heat. Add hana katsuo and let stand 2 minutes, then strain. Add aka miso and shiro miso. Stir well. Heat thoroughly but do not boil. Garnish and serve.

Princess Kaiulani Hotel
Honolulu, Hawaii

Artichoke Bowls   *Serves 6*

A unique soup that must be made ahead.

   6   fresh artichokes
12 ounces   French or Italian salad dressing
1 1/2 cups   chilled consommé
6 tablespoons   sour cream
3 tablespoons   caviar
sour cream for dipping

Cook artichokes until tender. Spread artichoke open and remove choke. Pour 1 to 2 tablespoons of salad dressing into the center of each artichoke. Let stand several hours or refrigerate overnight. Fill each artichoke with 1/4 cup chilled consommé. Top with 1 tablespoon of sour cream and 1/2 teaspoon of caviar. Serve on individual plates with additional sour cream for the leaves.

Hot and Sour Soup *Serves 6*

6 cups	chicken stock
1/3 pound	lean pork butt, slivered
6	dried mushrooms, soaked to soften and julienned
1/2 cup	bamboo shoots, julienned
1/2 cup	water chestnuts,* sliced
1 teaspoon	minced fresh ginger*
1/2 cup	cloud ears,* soaked to soften
1 pound	firm tofu,* cut into small cubes
1 tablespoon	soy sauce
1 tablespoon	rice wine*
2 tablespoons	rice vinegar*
1/2 teaspoon	white pepper
	salt to taste
1	egg, beaten
2 tablespoons	chopped green onion
1/2 teaspoon	sesame oil*
1/2 teaspoon	chili oil* (optional)

Bring stock to a boil, add pork, mushrooms, bamboo shoots, water chestnuts, ginger and cloud ears. Reduce heat and simmer for 10 minutes. Add tofu, soy sauce, rice wine, rice vinegar and pepper. Bring back to a boil. Season and remove from heat. Slowly pour in egg, stirring constantly. Add green onion, sesame oil and chili oil. Serve immediately.

Pork and Watercress Soup   *Serves 4*

         2 ounces   lean pork
          6 cups   chicken stock
         1/2 inch   fresh ginger,* sliced
1 1/2 tablespoons   sherry
       1/2 bunch   watercress, sliced
             1   green onion, thinly sliced
                 salt to taste

Cut pork across the grain into 1/4-inch slices and then into 1/8-inch strips. In a large pot, heat the stock almost to a boil. Add pork strips and ginger. Reduce heat, cover and simmer until meat is no longer pink, about 10 minutes. Discard ginger slices and skim the soup. Stir in the sherry. Add watercress and green onion. Simmer uncovered until watercress softens, but still retains its fresh green color, about 3 minutes. Season and serve.

Egg Drop Soup   *Serves 2*

1 (14 1/2-ounce) can   chicken broth
       1/2-inch   fresh ginger,* thinly sliced
        1 large   egg
                 *Garnish: Chopped green onions and Chinese parsley**

Heat chicken broth in a medium saucepan. Add ginger and simmer for 5 minutes. Discard ginger. Beat egg in a dish. Bring the soup to a rapid boil and pour in the beaten egg and stir immediately. Remove from heat and continue stirring until egg is barely cooked. (Do not overcook egg. It will become hard and not look lacy.) Garnish and serve.

106

Cold Banana Bisque with Cinnamon Croutons

Serves 8

This is a refreshing soup to serve at a brunch or luncheon.

1 quart	Half and Half
4 large	ripe bananas
dash	nutmeg

Put Half and Half, bananas and nutmeg in the blender and blend until thoroughly mixed and creamy. Chill.

Cinnamon Croutons

3 pieces	thinly sliced white bread
1/3 cup	melted butter
3 tablespoons	sugar
1/2 teaspoon	cinnamon

Preheat oven to 300 degrees. Remove crust, cube bread and place in a buttered shallow pan. Combine melted butter, sugar and cinnamon and pour over croutons. Toss until evenly coated. Bake, stirring frequently, until lightly caramelized. Sprinkle croutons on chilled soup and serve.

Papaya Soup

Serves 8

Can be served hot or cold. Best results occur with slightly under-ripe papaya.

1 medium	onion, thinly sliced
2 tablespoons	butter
1 large	papaya,* peeled and diced
3 cups	water
2 sprigs	parsley
1 teaspoon	salt
3 cups	milk
dash	mace
1 tablespoon	cornstarch
$1/4$ cup	water
$1^1/2$ cups	Half and Half

Garnish: Parsley and nutmeg

In a saucepan, sauté onion in butter for 5 minutes. Add papaya, water, parsley and salt. Simmer over low heat for 1 hour. Press mixture through a sieve and return to saucepan. Stir in milk and mace. Dissolve cornstarch in $1/4$ cup water and add to soup, stirring constantly. Simmer for 10 minutes. Do not boil. Add Half and Half and heat thoroughly. Garnish.

Chinese Chicken Lemon Soup

Serves 8 – 10

8 cups	chicken stock
3	chicken breasts, skinned
1	bay leaf
1	onion, peeled and quartered
1/2 cup	chopped celery
1/2 cup	grated carrot
	grated peel and juice of 1 lemon
	salt and pepper to taste
2 cups	fresh snow peas*
3 tablespoons	chopped green onion

Garnish: 1 lemon, thinly sliced

In a large pot, bring the chicken stock, chicken breasts, bay leaf, onion, celery, carrot, lemon juice and peel to a boil. Season, reduce heat and simmer for 1 hour. Remove chicken breasts from the stock and cool. Shred the chicken and discard the bones. Strain the stock through a fine sieve. One half hour before serving, add the chicken, snow peas and green onion. Reheat and serve. Garnish with thin slices of lemon.

Velvet Corn Soup
with Crab

Serves 10

1 tablespoon	vegetable oil
1/4 pound	ground pork
1 teaspoon	minced fresh ginger*
10 cups	chicken stock
2 tablespoons	sherry
12 ounces	creamed corn
3 tablespoons	cornstarch dissolved in 4 tablespoons of water
3	egg whites, slightly beaten
10 ounces	fresh or frozen crab, flaked
	salt and pepper to taste
	Garnish: 4 green onions, thinly sliced

In a large saucepan, sauté ground pork and ginger in oil. Add stock, sherry and corn and bring to a boil. Thicken with cornstarch-water mixture. Slowly stir in egg whites. Add crab and season. Remove from heat. Garnish and serve.

Pine Tree Mushroom Soup

2 large	fall pine mushrooms*
3/4 pound	tender beef
3	green onions, chopped diagonally
1 tablespoon	sesame seeds, toasted and pulverized
2 tablespoons	soy sauce
1 1/2 tablespoons	vegetable oil
12 cups	beef broth
1 tablespoon	soy sauce
1 teaspoon	sesame oil*

Soak mushrooms in water for 30 minutes. Drain and pat dry. Remove stems and slice in thin strips against the grain. Slice beef into thin strips. Combine meat, green onions, sesame seeds and soy sauce. Let stand for 15 minutes. Heat vegetable oil in large skillet. Add meat and marinade and cook for 3 minutes. Add mushrooms and cook for 2 minutes. Pour in beef broth and 1 tablespoon soy sauce and simmer until meat is tender. Add sesame oil just before serving.

Corn Chowder

1 pound	bacon
3 tablespoons	flour
1 cup	diced onion
1 cup	diced celery
1 cup	diced carrots
2 cups	diced potatoes
1 quart	milk
1 (17-ounce) can	cream style corn
2 teaspoons	salt
1/2 teaspoon	white pepper
1 teaspoon	Worcestershire sauce

Garnish: Chopped parsley

Dice and fry the bacon. Pour off all but 2 tablespoons of drippings. Add flour to bacon. Stir and turn off heat. Combine onion, celery, carrots and potatoes in a saucepan and barely cover with water. Cook for 10 minutes. Add water and vegetables to bacon and cook another 10 minutes. Stir in milk, corn, salt, pepper and Worcestershire. Bring ingredients to a boil. Garnish and serve. Variation: 1 cup grated Cheddar cheese or Gruyère cheese may be stirred in before serving.

Albert Schmid
Executive Chef
Dillingham Corporation
Honolulu, Hawaii

112

Yam Yam Soup

Serves 4 — 6

An unusual and spicy soup to be served hot or cold.

1 pound	yams
1/2 tablespoon	grated orange peel
1 teaspoon	Chinese Five Spice*
1 teaspoon	cinnamon
1 teaspoon	ground ginger
1/8 teaspoon	cayenne
	salt and white pepper to taste
1/3 cup	orange juice
1 1/2 cups	chicken broth
1 1/2 cups	Half and Half

Garnish: Toasted coconut

Boil yams until soft. Cool and peel. Place yams, seasonings, chicken broth and Half and Half in blender. Blend until smooth. (Best if done in small batches.) To serve cold, refrigerate for several hours. To serve hot, heat but do not bring to a boil. Garnish. Note: Soup may be thinned with equal parts of chicken broth and Half and Half.

Fresh Mushroom Bisque *Serves 6*

1/2 pound	butter
3/4 pound	fresh mushrooms, sliced
1 clove	garlic, minced
1/2 cup	chopped onion
2 tablespoons	lemon juice
4 tablespoons	flour
4 cups	chicken broth
1 1/2 teaspoons	salt
1/4 teaspoon	pepper
2 cups	Half and Half

Garnish: Fresh parsley

Sauté mushrooms, garlic and onion in butter for 3 minutes. Add lemon juice. Mix flour in a small amount of the chicken broth to prevent lumps and add along with the remaining ingredients to the mushroom mixture. Simmer for 15 minutes. Do not boil. Garnish and serve.

Chinese Oxtail Soup

5 pounds	oxtails, cut in sections
1/2 cup	raw shelled peanuts, blanched
3 (14-ounce) cans	beef broth (chicken broth may be substituted)
1 small piece	kwo pee*
1 clove	garlic, minced
1/2 – 1 inch piece	fresh ginger,* peeled and crushed
1 small piece	star anise* (approximately 3 spokes)
2	green onions
1 stalk	celery
1/4 cup	whiskey
1/2 teaspoon	salt
1/2 teaspoon	garlic salt
1 cup	fresh watercress, cut in 2-inch pieces

Garnish: Minced green onions, minced Chinese parsley,* grated fresh ginger*

In a large pot, parboil oxtails in water for 5 minutes. Drain. Add remaining ingredients except for watercress and garnish. Cover and simmer for 3 hours or until oxtails are tender. Remove and discard green onions and celery. Chill soup overnight (or in freezer for a few hours) and remove congealed fat. Add watercress and reheat before serving. Garnish.

Spicy Gazpacho

Serves 10

3 (1-pound 12-ounce) cans	whole tomatoes, drained (approximately 6 cups)
1	onion, chopped
1/2 cup	chopped green pepper
1/2 – 1 cup	chopped cucumber
1 clove	garlic, minced
1/2 teaspoon	ground cumin
1 tablespoon	salt
	freshly ground black pepper
2 cups	tomato juice or V-8 juice
1/4 cup	olive oil
1/4 – 1/2 cup	white wine vinegar

Garnish: 1/2 cup each chopped onion, green pepper, cucumber, Garlic Croutons (see index).

Put the tomatoes, onion, green pepper, cucumber and spices in blender or food processor and blend. Transfer to a large bowl and stir in tomato juice. Cover and chill. Stir in oil and vinegar before serving. Garnish to taste. Variation: Add 1/2 — 1 teaspoon Worcestershire sauce for a spicier taste.

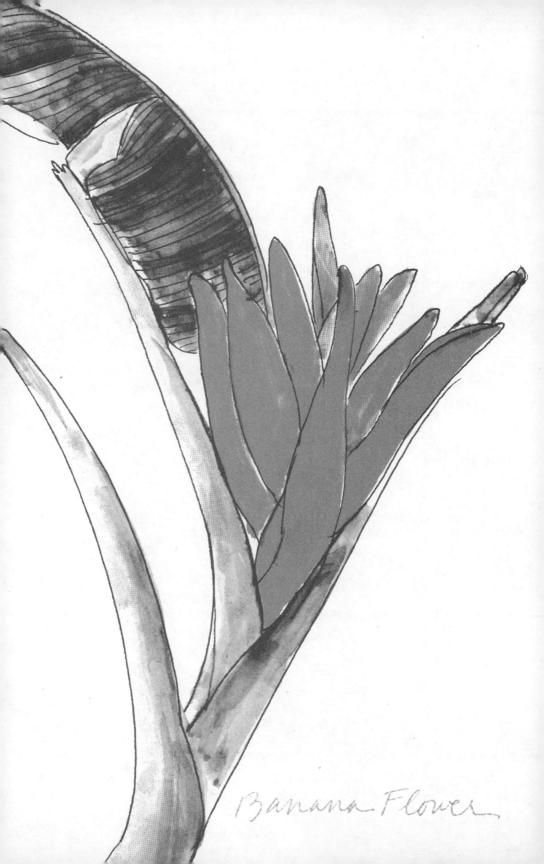

Banana Flower

Breads

Macadamia Nut Crescents

Makes 24 crescents

Filling

2 tablespoons	butter
2 tablespoons	brown sugar
2/3 cup	chopped macadamia nuts*

Cream butter and sugar. Add nuts and blend well. Set aside.

Dough

1 package (1 tablespoon)	active dry yeast
1/4 cup	lukewarm water
2 cups	flour
2 tablespoons	sugar
2/3 cup	butter
1	egg
1	egg white, beaten until frothy
	sugar

Soften yeast in lukewarm water. Sift flour and sugar into a bowl and cut in butter with a pastry blender until mixture resembles coarse cornmeal. Stir egg and yeast into mixture. Work dough with floured hands until smooth. Cover and let rise for 1 hour. Divide dough into two equal parts. Roll each into an 11-inch circle. Cut into 12 wedges. Put 1 tablespoon of filling at the widest end of each wedge. Roll from widest point into a crescent shape and place on greased cookie sheet. Brush with egg white. Let crescents rise at room temperature for 1 hour. Preheat oven to 400 degrees. Sprinkle with sugar and bake 8 to 10 minutes or until golden. Note: If macadamia nuts are not available, pecans, almonds or walnuts may be substituted.

120

Punahou Malasadas   *Makes 5 dozen*

At their carnival, Punahou School sells 85,000 malasadas* in just two days.

1 package (1 tablespoon)	active dry yeast
1 teaspoon	sugar
1/4 cup	warm water
6 cups	flour
1/2 cup	sugar
1/2 teaspoon	salt
1/4 cup	melted butter
6	eggs
1 cup	evaporated milk
1 cup	water
	vegetable oil for deep frying
	sugar and dash of nutmeg

Mix yeast with 1 teaspoon sugar and add to warm water. Let stand for 5 minutes. Sift dry ingredients together. Stir in melted butter. Beat eggs, milk and water together and add to flour mixture. Add yeast and mix well. Dough will be sticky. Cover and let dough rise until doubled, then punch down. Let dough rise a second time. Heat oil in deep fryer to 375 degrees. Dip fingertips in bowl or oil or softened butter then pinch off golf ball size pieces of raised dough. Drop in heated oil and cook until golden brown on one side. Turn over and fry until golden on the other side. Drain on paper towels and roll in sugar-nutmeg mixture. Serve immediately. Note: This recipe doubles well.

Longhi's Cinnamon Rolls

Makes 18 – 20 rolls

1/2 cup	warm water
1 package (1 tablespoon)	active dry yeast
3 tablespoons	sugar
2/3 cup	milk, scalded and cooled
1/4 cup	melted butter
2	eggs
1/2 teaspoon	salt
2 1/2 cups	flour
2 cups	whole wheat flour
1/4 cup	melted butter
1/2 cup	raisins, soaked in water until softened
2/3 cup	brown sugar, firmly packed
1 1/2 tablespoons	cinnamon
1/2 – 3/4 cup	chopped pecans (optional)

Combine water and yeast, stirring until dissolved. Add sugar and let stand 15 to 20 minutes or until yeast begins to bubble. Combine yeast mixture, milk, butter, eggs and salt in a large bowl and mix well. Add flour to make a stiff dough. Cover and let rise until doubled. Punch down dough. Roll dough on lightly floured surface into 23 x 14-inch rectangle. Brush with melted butter and sprinkle with raisins. Combine brown sugar, cinnamon and pecans and sprinkle over dough. Roll into cylinder shape as for jelly roll. Slice dough into 1 to 1 1/2-inch strips. Place rolls flat on greased baking sheets or in three 8-inch square pans. Cover and let rise in warm place until double in size, approximately 30 to 45 minutes. Preheat oven to 350 degrees. Bake for 20 to 25 minutes. Brush with butter and drizzle with icing.

continued...

Icing

1¹/2 – 2 cups	powdered sugar
2 tablespoons	light corn syrup
	juice of 1 orange or lemon

Combine powdered sugar, corn syrup and juice. Blend until smooth.

Longhi's Restaurant
Lahaina, Maui

Dutch Baby   *Serves 4*

This fluffy oven pancake cooks in a large frying pan.

¹/4 cup	butter
3	eggs
³/4 cup	milk
³/4 cup	flour

Preheat oven to 425 degrees. Melt butter in a 2 to 3-quart frying pan or shallow baking dish. Whirl eggs for one minute in blender, gradually adding milk and flour. Pour batter into hot buttered pan and bake for 20 to 25 minutes. Serve immediately with your choice of toppings: powdered sugar and lemon juice, honey, syrup, jams and jellies, fresh fruit, or heated fruits. Note: This recipe doubles well. Use a 5-quart pan.

Tutu's Kuchen

Grandmother's delicious holiday coffee cake.

1 cup	milk, scalded and cooled to lukewarm
1 package (1 tablespoon)	active dry yeast
4 tablespoons	shortening
2 tablespoons	sugar
2	eggs, beaten
1/2 teaspoon	salt
3 1/4 cups	sifted flour
4 tablespoons	melted butter
1/2 cup	sugar
2 teaspoons	cinnamon
	candied fruit, crushed pineapple, chopped nuts, raisins

Grease a 10-inch tube pan. Add yeast to lukewarm milk, stirring until dissolved. In a mixing bowl, cream shortening and sugar. Add eggs, cooled milk, salt and flour, blending well. Place bowl in a warm place and let rise until doubled in size. Punch down. Pinch off pieces of dough and form walnut-sized balls. Dip balls into melted butter, then roll thoroughly in sugar and cinnamon mixture. Layer balls in pan, sprinkling fruits and nuts throughout. Let rise 1 hour. Preheat oven to 350 degrees. Bake for 30 to 40 minutes. Cool for a few minutes before turning out on a serving platter. To serve, pull apart.

Coconut Cinnamon Sour Cream Coffee Cake

Serves 10 – 12

1 cup	butter
2 cups	sugar
2 cups	flour
1/4 teaspoon	salt
1 teaspoon	baking powder
3	eggs
1 teaspoon	vanilla
1 cup	sour cream
1 1/2 cups	flaked coconut

Spice filling

1 cup	chopped pecans
3 – 4 teaspoons	cinnamon
6 tablespoons	brown sugar
1/2 – 3/4 cup	flaked coconut

Preheat oven to 325 degrees. Grease bundt pan. Cream butter and sugar. Sift dry ingredients and add to creamed mixture, alternating with eggs. Stir in vanilla, sour cream and coconut. In a separate bowl, combine filling ingredients. Pour half of the batter into bundt pan, then add half of the filling mixture. Add remaining batter and sprinkle balance of filling on top. Bake for 1 1/4 to 1 1/2 hours.

Old-Fashioned Waffles

Serves 4

Lightest, fluffiest, tastiest waffles in the world!

2 cups	sifted flour
1 teaspoon	baking soda
3/4 teaspoon	salt
1 tablespoon	sugar
2 teaspoons	baking powder
3	egg yolks, beaten
2 cups	buttermilk
3	egg whites, stiffly beaten
1/3 cup	warm bacon drippings, from approximately 8 strips of bacon

Preheat waffle iron. Combine flour, baking soda, salt, sugar and baking powder. In a separate bowl, mix egg yolks with buttermilk. Gradually add egg yolk mixture to dry ingredients, beating constantly until smooth. Fold in stiffly beaten egg whites. Add warm bacon drippings. Mix until blended. Ladle batter onto waffle iron and bake until golden.

Sunshine Orange Crêpes *Serves 6*

1 cup	flour
1/4 cup	melted butter
5	eggs
1 3/4 cups	milk
1/2 cup	sugar
1/2 teaspoon	salt
	grated peel of 1 orange
	grated peel of 1 lemon
	butter

Combine flour and butter until smooth. Add eggs and mix well. Add milk, sugar, salt and grated peel and stir until blended. Melt a small amount of butter in crêpe pan until pan is coated. Cook individual crêpes, recoating pan with butter as needed. Set crêpes aside.

Orange Filling

1 cup	butter, melted
1 cup	powdered sugar
	grated peel of 1 orange, reserve
	orange juice

Beat butter and sugar until frothy. Add grated peel. Fill individual crêpes with orange filling. Fold crêpes and place seam side down on serving platter. Squeeze a little orange juice over the top of each crêpe and serve.

Boston Brown Bread

Makes 3 loaves

2 cups	boiling water
1 cup	raisins
2 tablespoons	butter
1 cup	brown sugar
1 cup	sugar
2	eggs, beaten
1 teaspoon	vanilla
3/4 cup	chopped walnuts
2 cups	flour
2 cups	graham flour
2 teaspoons	baking soda
1 tablespoon	salt

Preheat oven to 350 degrees. Grease inside of three 26 1/2-ounce tin cans with vegetable oil. Pour boiling water over raisins. Stir in butter and sugars. Cool. Add eggs, vanilla and walnuts. In a separate large bowl, combine flours, soda and salt. Add the raisin mixture and blend thoroughly. Spoon batter into each can, about two-thirds full. Bake for 1 hour. When done, carefully shake bread out of cans and place immediately in a plastic bag. Seal the bag to allow the bread to steam. Serve as is or chilled with cream cheese.

Mmmm Good
Mango Bread

Makes 1 loaf

2 cups	flour
2 teaspoons	baking soda
1½ teaspoons	salt
2 teaspoons	cinnamon
3	eggs
½ cup	vegetable oil
1½ cups	sugar
1 teaspoon	vanilla
½ cup	golden raisins
½ cup	chopped nuts
2 cups	diced mango*
¼ cup	flaked coconut (optional)

Preheat oven to 350 degrees. Grease a one pound loaf pan or a bundt pan. Sift flour, soda, salt and cinnamon into large mixing bowl. Make a well and add the remaining ingredients, mixing thoroughly. Pour into pan and let stand for 20 minutes. Bake for 1 hour.

Mango Bread

Makes 3 small loaves

Freeze mango purée for use when mangoes are out of season.

2 cups	mango* purée (papaya* purée or
	papaya yogurt may be substituted)
1 cup	vegetable oil
3	eggs
1 teaspoon	vanilla
	grated peel of 1 orange (optional)
2 cups	flour (may use 1 cup whole wheat,
	1 cup all purpose)
2 teaspoons	baking soda
1/2 teaspoon	salt
1 1/2 cups	sugar
1/4 teaspoon	ground cloves
1/2 teaspoon	pumpkin pie spice (optional)
1/4 teaspoon	nutmeg
2 teaspoons	cinnamon
1 cup	bran buds or granola
1 cup	raisins
1 cup	chopped nuts (optional)
1/2 cup	shredded coconut (optional)

Preheat oven to 350 degrees. Grease three 3 x 7-inch loaf pans. In a blender, blend mango purée, oil, eggs, vanilla and orange peel. Sift flour, baking powder and salt. Add sugar and spices. Combine mango mixture with dry ingredients. Stir in raisins, nuts and coconut. Spoon mixture almost to top of pans. Bake for one hour or until done.

Banana Lemon
Tea Bread

Serves 12 — 14

2/3 cup	shortening
1 cup	sugar
2	eggs
1 1/2 cups	mashed ripe bananas
6 tablespoons	lemon juice
2 cups	flour
1 teaspoon	baking soda
1 teaspoon	salt
1 tablespoon	grated lemon peel

Preheat oven to 350 degrees. Grease a bundt pan or two medium loaf pans. Cream shortening and sugar. Blend in eggs, bananas and lemon juice. Sift dry ingredients and stir into batter. Add grated lemon peel. Pour into prepared pan and bake for one hour.

Banana Nut Bread

Makes 1 loaf

The staple of Sunday brunches, everyday lunches and the most common way of dealing with a bumper backyard banana explosion!

$1/2$ cup	sugar
$1/2$ cup	brown sugar
$1/2$ cup	butter
2	eggs
2 cups	flour
$1/2$ teaspoon	baking powder
$1/2$ teaspoon	salt
3 tablespoons	buttermilk
1 teaspoon	baking soda
3 – 4	bananas, mashed
1 cup	chopped pecans
1 teaspoon	vanilla

Preheat oven to 350 degrees. Grease a one-pound loaf pan, bundt pan or muffin tins. Cream sugars and butter. Blend in eggs. Sift dry ingredients and add to batter. Combine buttermilk and soda and stir into batter. Add mashed bananas, nuts and vanilla. Pour into prepared pan and bake for 45 minutes. Variation: This recipe will make 24 to 30 muffins. Baking time is reduced to 15 minutes.

Tropical Nut Bread

Makes 1 loaf

2 cups	flour
1 teaspoon	baking soda
2 teaspoons	baking powder
$^1/_2$ teaspoon	salt
1 ($8^1/_4$-ounce) can	crushed pineapple, undrained
1 cup	mashed banana
$^1/_3$ cup	orange juice
$^1/_2$ cup	butter
1 cup	sugar
2	eggs, beaten
$1^1/_2 - 2$ cups	chopped macadamia nuts*

Preheat oven to 350 degrees. Butter a one-pound loaf pan. Sift dry ingredients together and set aside. Combine pineapple, banana and orange juice and set aside. In a large bowl, cream butter and sugar. Add eggs and beat well. Add a small amount of the flour mixture alternately with the fruit mixture, mixing only enough to moisten the flour. Stir in nuts and pour batter into pan. Bake for 1 hour 15 minutes. Note: This bread is much better after a day or two.

133

Lemon Bread

Makes 1 loaf

6 tablespoons	butter
1 cup	sugar
1$^{1}/_{2}$ teaspoons	grated lemon peel
2	eggs
1$^{1}/_{2}$ cups	flour
1 teaspoon	baking powder
$^{1}/_{2}$ teaspoon	salt
$^{1}/_{2}$ cup	milk
1 cup	chopped walnuts or pecans

Glaze

1 tablespoon	lemon juice
$^{1}/_{2}$ cup	powdered sugar

Preheat oven to 350 degrees. Grease a one-pound loaf pan. Cream butter and sugar and add grated lemon peel. Add eggs and blend well. Stir in dry ingredients and milk. Add nuts. Pour batter into pan and bake for 55 minutes. Cool slightly. Remove from pan. Combine glaze ingredients and pour over the bread while it is still warm.

Zucchini Bread

Makes 2 loaves

3	eggs
2 cups	sugar
1 cup	vegetable oil
2 cups	grated raw zucchini
3 teaspoons	vanilla
3 cups	flour
1 teaspoon	salt
1 teaspoon	baking soda
1/4 teaspoon	baking powder
3 teaspoons	cinnamon
1 cup	chopped walnuts (optional)

Preheat oven to 350 degrees. Butter 2 one-pound loaf pans. Beat eggs until light and foamy. Add sugar, oil, zucchini and vanilla. Do not overmix. Combine dry ingredients and stir into zucchini mixture. Add nuts and pour into pans. Bake for 60 minutes. Cool on wire rack.

Garlic Croutons

Makes 3—4 cups

6 slices	white bread, dry or lightly toasted
1/2 cup	clarified butter
2 cloves	garlic, minced

Remove crusts and cut bread into 1/2-inch squares. Sauté the garlic in butter for 2 minutes over medium heat. Add bread cubes and stir until crisp and golden. Drain on a paper towel.

135

Gougère

Serves 8 – 10

A novel cheese bread, excellent with salad and gazpacho.

1/2 cup	butter
1 cup	flour
4	eggs, beaten
3/4 pound	Swiss cheese, grated
1/4 pound	Cheddar cheese, grated
1/4 teaspoon	salt
1/4 teaspoon	pepper

Preheat oven to 375 degrees. Melt butter and add flour, mixing well. Slowly add eggs. Stir in cheese, salt and pepper. Spread in lightly greased 10-inch skillet and bake for 45 minutes. Cool and slice in pie-shaped wedges. Note: This can be prepared in a food processor.

Crêpe Batter

Makes 24 crêpes

This recipe can be used for both dessert and entrée crêpes.

3	eggs
2 tablespoons	sugar
1 teaspoon	vanilla
dash	salt
1 1/2 cups	milk
1/4 cup	beer
1 cup	flour
2 – 3 tablespoons	melted butter

Combine ingredients in a blender and blend until smooth. Chill. Heat a 6 or 7-inch crêpe pan and coat with butter. When pan is hot, pour about 2 tablespoons batter into pan and tilt to spread evenly. Cook approximately 30 seconds or until lightly browned. Turn crêpe and cook for about 15 seconds. Recoat pan with butter as needed. Note: Freeze crêpes between layers of wax paper and wrap in tin foil.

Lavosh

Serves 6—8

2³/4 cups   flour
1/2 teaspoon   baking soda
1/2 teaspoon   salt
1/4 cup   sugar
1/2 cup   butter
1 cup   buttermilk
   lightly toasted sesame seeds
   poppy seeds

Preheat oven to 375 degrees. Lightly grease a cookie sheet. Sift dry ingredients together. Cut in butter. Add buttermilk and mix until batter forms a big ball. Pinch off tablespoon-size balls of dough. Flour a cutting board and sprinkle with sesame and poppy seeds. Roll out each ball of dough until it is quite thin. Pick up rolled dough on rolling pin and place on cookie sheet. Repeat process of flouring the cutting board and sprinkling with seeds as needed. Bake each batch for 6 to 8 minutes or until golden brown.

Icebox Bran Muffins   *Makes 2¹/2 dozen*

1 cup	All-Bran cereal
1 cup	boiling water
¹/2 cup	shortening
1¹/2 cups	sugar
2	eggs, beaten
2 cups	buttermilk
2¹/2 cups	sifted flour
2¹/2 teaspoons	baking soda
¹/2 teaspoon	salt
2¹/2 cups	All-Bran cereal

Preheat oven to 400 degrees. Soak 1 cup of All-Bran in boiling water and set aside. Cream shortening and sugar. Add eggs, buttermilk and soaked bran. Add flour, baking soda and salt. Fold in dry bran until ingredients are moistened. Spoon into greased muffin tins and bake for 20 to 25 minutes. Note: This recipe doubles very well and batter may be stored in the refrigerator for one month. For variety, try adding dates, raisins, nuts, blueberries or chopped apples.

Lychee

Meats

Entrées

Beef Tomato

Serves 6

Colorful vegetables accent this Oriental dish.

1 pound	top sirloin, sliced into $1/4$-inch strips
$1/2$ pound	pork, sliced into $1/4$-inch strips
5 tablespoons	soy sauce
3 tablespoons	cornstarch
2 teaspoons	brown sugar
2 tablespoons	vegetable oil
1 tablespoon	minced fresh ginger*
2 cloves	garlic, minced
	salt and pepper
1 tablespoon	vegetable oil
2 medium	onions, cut in wedges
2 stalks	celery, sliced diagonally
2	green peppers, sliced
$1^{1/2}$ cups	sliced fresh mushrooms
4 medium	tomatoes, quartered
2	green onions, chopped

Combine soy sauce, cornstarch, brown sugar, oil, ginger, garlic, salt and pepper. Marinate meat for 15 minutes. Heat oil in wok.* Drain meat, reserving marinade, and brown in wok. Remove meat. Add oil if needed and stir-fry onions, celery, green peppers and mushrooms. Return meat to pan. Add marinade, tomatoes and green onion. Heat thoroughly and serve over rice.

Beef Tenderloin
Stuffed with Lobster

Serves 8

3 – 4 pound	whole beef tenderloin, butterflied
2 (4-ounce)	lobster tails
1 tablespoon	melted butter
1 1/2 teaspoons	lemon juice
6 slices	bacon, partially cooked
1/2 cup	sliced green onion
1/2 cup	butter
1/2 cup	dry white wine
1/8 teaspoon	garlic salt

Garnish: Whole mushrooms and watercress

Preheat oven to 425 degrees. Bring lobster tails to a boil in salted water and cover. Reduce heat and simmer for 5 to 6 minutes. Cut lobster tails in half lengthwise and remove meat. Place lobster end to end inside beef. Combine 1 tablespoon butter and lemon juice and drizzle over lobster. Tie roast together securely at 1-inch intervals. Place on a rack in a shallow roasting pan. Roast for 45 minutes for rare beef and 1 hour for well done. Lay bacon strips on top of roast and bake for 5 minutes. In a saucepan, simmer green onion in 1/2 cup butter until tender. Stir in wine and garlic salt and bring to a boil. To serve, slice roast and spoon on wine sauce. Garnish platter with fluted whole mushrooms and watercress.

Filet Charlemagne *Serves 4*

2 pound	beef tenderloin
1/4 teaspoon	salt
1/4 teaspoon	pepper
1/4 teaspoon	rosemary
1/4 teaspoon	thyme
4 tablespoons	vegetable oil

Preheat oven to 350 degrees. Season beef with herbs and spices. Brown well in oil and bake for 25 to 30 minutes. Serve with Sauce Charlemagne.

Sauce Charlemagne

2 tablespoons	butter
1/2 cup	white wine
	juice of 1 lemon
1 pound	fresh mushrooms, quartered
2 tablespoons	cornstarch
1 cup	whipping cream
	salt and pepper

Combine butter, wine and lemon juice in a saucepan. Bring to a boil and add the mushrooms. Reduce heat and simmer for 5 minutes. Remove mushrooms and set aside. Add cornstarch to sauce, using a whisk to avoid lumps. Stir in cream and mushrooms. Season to taste.

The Third Floor
Hawaiian Regent Hotel
Honolulu, Hawaii

Tournedos Mitchell   *Serves 1*

2 (3½-ounce)	beef tenderloin filets
1 ounce	mushrooms, sliced
2 medium	shrimp
2 ounces	clarified butter
1 teaspoon	fresh basil
½ teaspoon	seasoning salt
1 ounce	white wine
4 ounces	béarnaise sauce
	Garnish: Chopped parsley and paprika

Broil filets to desired degree of doneness. In a saucepan, melt butter and sauté mushrooms and shrimp with basil, seasoning salt and wine. Pour mixture over filets. Glaze with béarnaise sauce. Garnish with chopped parsley and paprika.

Alfred "Almar" Arcano
Executive Chef
Hy's Steak House
Honolulu, Hawaii

London Broil

Serves 4

1¹/₂ – 2 pound	London Broil
1¹/₂ – 2 teaspoons	salt
1 teaspoon	sugar
1 tablespoon	minced onion
¹/₂ teaspoon	dry mustard
¹/₂ teaspoon	rosemary
¹/₂ teaspoon	ground ginger
1 teaspoon	whole peppercorns
3 cloves	garlic, sliced
¹/₄ cup	lemon juice
¹/₂ cup	vegetable oil

Combine seasonings, lemon juice and oil and marinate meat in refrigerator for 3 to 4 hours, turning occasionally. Remove from marinade and broil for 5 to 10 minutes on each side. Slice across the grain.

Pulehu Ribs

Serves 4

Pulehu means "to broil" in Hawaiian.

3 pounds	beef short ribs
1 tablespoon	sugar
1 tablespoon	Hawaiian rock salt*
1¹/₂ tablespoons	soy sauce
1¹/₂ teaspoons	Chili Pepper Water* (see index)
1 teaspoon	sesame oil*

Combine ingredients and rub into ribs. Let stand for 3 to 4 hours. Grill over charcoal.

Easy Picnic Short Ribs *Serves 4*

With miles of sandy beaches, picnics are a popular pastime in Hawaii.

2 pounds	thin-sliced beef short ribs

Sauce/Marinade:

1/3 cup	soy sauce
1 tablespoon	mirin*
1 tablespoon	olive oil
2 cloves	garlic, crushed
1 tablespoon	chopped green onion
2 teaspoons	sugar

Combine ingredients and marinate ribs for 2 hours. Sauce may be used to baste ribs while barbecuing if there is not sufficient time to marinate the ribs.

Smoked Brisket *Serves 6—8*

Excellent with potato salad and baked beans. Reheat the next day with barbecue sauce for a change of flavor.

3 – 5 pound	beef brisket
1 (3 1/2-ounce) bottle	liquid smoke
1 teaspoon	garlic salt
1 1/2 teaspoons	Beau Monde
3/4 teaspoon	black pepper
1/2 teaspoon	onion salt
2 teaspoons	Worcestershire sauce

Preheat oven to 275 degrees. Place brisket on a large piece of heavy duty foil. Add seasonings and wrap foil tightly around brisket. Place on rimmed baking sheet and bake for 4 to 5 hours. To serve, slice against the grain or shred.

Korean Barbecued Hamburgers

Serves 4

A new way to serve an old stand-by.

1/3 cup	soy sauce
3 tablespoons	sugar
2 tablespoons	toasted sesame seed
1 tablespoon	vegetable oil
1/2 cup	chopped onion
1/3 cup	minced green onion
1 pound	lean ground beef

Combine ingredients and refrigerate for 1 hour or more. Shape into 4 to 6 patties and grill. Serve on hamburger buns.

Kalbi

Serves 4

Distinctly Korean, these ribs are a popular barbecue entrée.

2 – 3 pounds	beef short ribs
3/4 cup	soy sauce
3/4 cup	sugar
3/4 cup	water
3-inch piece	fresh ginger,* sliced
1 clove	garlic, minced
1 tablespoon	sesame oil*

Combine ingredients and marinate ribs for 4 hours. Broil or barbecue.

Classical Korean Dried Beef

Serves 8 — 10

This dish is usually garnished with dried cuttlefish, cut in artistic shapes.

1 pound	beef round steak
4 tablespoons	soy sauce
2 teaspoons	dry white wine
1 tablespoon	sugar
1 teaspoon	garlic juice
1/8 teaspoon	fresh ginger juice*
1/4 teaspoon	pepper
2 tablespoons	peanut oil
1 teaspoon	sesame oil*
	Garnish: Pine nuts and dried cuttlefish *

Slice beef across grain into 1/8-inch strips and place in a bowl. Combine soy sauce, wine, sugar, garlic juice, ginger juice and pepper. Add to meat. Spread beef slices on a wire rack and dry in the sun. Turn often until dried. (Meat will take 1 to 3 days to dry.) For a richer color, brush a combination of peanut and sesame oil lightly over the meat slices. When dried, broil over charcoal and cut into serving pieces. Serve on a platter and garnish with nuts and dried cuttlefish. Note: Dried cuttlefish can easily be carved into shapes such as flowers and birds.

Hot Mongolian Beef   *Serves 4*

1/2 pound	flank steak
1	egg
1 tablespoon	water
1 tablespoon	cornstarch
5 cups	vegetable oil
1/4 ounce	long rice*
1/4 pound	carrot, shredded
1/4 pound	bell pepper, shredded
3 cloves	garlic, minced
1 teaspoon	minced fresh ginger*
6 – 7	Hawaiian chili peppers*
1 teaspoon	cooking wine
1 tablespoon	soy sauce
1 teaspoon	sugar

Thinly slice beef. Combine egg, water and cornstarch. Add beef, stir and let stand for 2 hours. Heat wok* until hot. Add oil and let stand for 10 seconds. Deep fry long rice to puff, and place on platter. Put beef into wok. Separate beef with a ladle until half-cooked. Add carrot and bell pepper. Stir until oil starts boiling. Drain, reserve leftover oil. Add garlic, ginger, chili peppers, wine, soy sauce and sugar. Stir 5 seconds, put drained beef into wok, stir and flip several times. Serve over crispy long rice.

Howard Co
Yen King Restaurant
Honolulu, Hawaii

Steak Tartare

8 ounces	extra lean ground beef
1	egg
1 teaspoon	Worcestershire sauce
dash	Tabasco
dash	salt
1 tablespoon	Mustard Mayonnaise (see index)
1 teaspoon	cracked green pepper
1 tablespoon	chopped red onion
1 tablespoon	chopped green pepper
1 tablespoon	chopped tomato
1 teaspoon	capers
1 teaspoon	sliced green olives

Garnish: Lettuce leaf, lemon wedges, cucumber slices, black olive and parsley

Combine beef, egg, Worcestershire, Tabasco and salt. Form into oblong patty and place on lettuce leaf on plate. Spread with Mustard Mayonnaise and top with a thin layer of cracked pepper, onions, green pepper, tomato, capers and green olives. Garnish with two lemon wedges at one end of patty and two cucumber slices at other end (dip one in paprika for color). Top cucumbers with black olive and parsley. Serve with melba toast.

Lois Canlis
Canlis' Restaurant
Honolulu, Hawaii

Beef with
Crisp Long Rice

Serves 4 — 6

Marinade:

2 tablespoons	cornstarch
1 teaspoon	grated fresh ginger*
1/2 teaspoon	salt
1 tablespoon	sugar
3 tablespoons	soy sauce

Combine ingredients and set aside.

1 pound	round steak, cut into 2-inch strips
1 cup	vegetable oil
14 ounces	long rice,* cut into 3-inch pieces
3/4 pound	shredded lettuce
1 clove	garlic
1-inch piece	fresh ginger,* thinly sliced
1 cup	sliced onions
2 teaspoons	cornstarch
1/2 teaspoon	salt
1 tablespoon	soy sauce
3/4 cup	water

Marinate round steak for 10 to 15 minutes. Heat oil in a large skillet and deep fry long rice a few pieces at a time for a few seconds until long rice puffs up. Drain on paper towels. Line a serving platter with lettuce and arrange long rice on top. Remove oil from skillet, reserving 1/4 cup. Add reserved oil, garlic and ginger to the skillet. Fry until browned and discard. Fry onions until limp and remove. Stir-fry the marinated beef for 2 minutes. Stir in the onions. Spoon the beef mixture over the long rice. Bring cornstarch, salt, soy sauce and water to a boil. Pour over the beef and serve immediately.

Baked Stuffed Papaya *Serves 8*

Wonderful as a luncheon dish or evening main course served with a light green salad and rolls.

1 medium	onion, chopped
1 medium	green pepper, seeded and chopped
1/4 cup	peanut oil
1 1/2 pounds	ground beef
3 cloves	garlic, minced
1 (16-ounce) can	whole tomatoes, drained and chopped
1/2 cup	tomato sauce
1	Hawaiian chili pepper,* seeded and minced
1/2 teaspoon	thyme
	salt and pepper
4	papayas* (about 1 pound each), cut in half and seeded
	salt and pepper
1/2 – 3/4 cup	grated Parmesan cheese

Preheat oven to 350 degrees. Sauté onion and green pepper in oil in a large skillet until onion is translucent. Add beef and garlic, breaking up meat and cooking until browned. Add tomatoes, tomato sauce, pepper and thyme, season to taste with salt and pepper. Reduce heat and simmer for 10 minutes until most of the liquid evaporates. Place papaya in 9 x 13-inch baking dish and sprinkle lightly with salt and pepper. Spoon beef mixture into papaya halves. Pour hot water into baking dish to a depth of 1 inch. Bake until papaya is tender, about 50 minutes. Sprinkle with cheese and bake for 15 minutes.

Prize Winning Chili   *Serves 12*

Great for tail-gate parties at Aloha Stadium.

1 cup	chopped onion
1/2 cup	chopped celery
2 pounds	ground beef
1 clove	garlic, minced
1 (2¹/4-ounce) package	chili seasoning
4 cups canned	whole tomatoes with liquid
1/2 teaspoon	salt
1¹/2 teaspoons	chili powder
1/2 teaspoon	pepper
1/2 teaspoon	garlic salt
1 teaspoon	ground cumin
1 (23-ounce) can	pinto beans

Sauté onions, celery, ground beef and garlic in skillet until ground beef is browned. Drain off fat and put meat mixture in Dutch oven. Add chili seasoning, tomatoes, salt, chili powder, pepper, garlic salt and cumin. Simmer for 30 minutes. Add beans and simmer for 15 minutes.

Veal Emincé

9 ounces	veal, thinly sliced
	salt and white pepper
1 tablespoon	flour
2 tablespoons	butter
1½ tablespoons	finely chopped onion
2 ounces	fresh mushrooms, sliced
¼ cup	white wine
½ cup	whipping cream
¼ cup	brown sauce or au jus

Garnish: Chopped parsley

Season veal with salt and pepper and sprinkle with flour. Quickly, sauté in butter until slightly browned on all sides. Remove veal. Add onions and mushrooms and sauté for 1 minute. Add white wine, cream and brown sauce and simmer for 1 minute more. Add veal to sauce. Heat thoroughly, but do not boil. Sprinkle with chopped parsley. Note: Serve with Roësti Potatoes (see index).

Martin Wyss
The Swiss Inn
Honolulu, Hawaii

Rahm Schnitzel *Serves 6*

2 pounds	veal cutlets, cut into ¼-inch slices
1 cup	lemon juice
	salt and pepper
	flour
4 tablespoons	butter
4 tablespoons	vegetable oil
2 cups	fresh mushrooms
1 cup	whipping cream

Marinate cutlets in lemon juice for 1 hour, turning every twenty minutes. Remove cutlets, pat dry and season. Dip in flour. In a large skillet, sauté veal in butter and oil for 8 to 10 minutes. Place veal on a large platter and keep warm in the oven. Reserve 1 tablespoon drippings in skillet and sauté mushrooms for 3 minutes. Add cream and bring to a boil, stirring until the sauce thickens. Pour sauce over veal and serve.

Pork Chops Indonesian

6 (1-inch)	loin pork chops
	salt and pepper
3 tablespoons	vegetable oil
1 (16-ounce) can	sliced peaches
2 tablespoons	brown sugar
1 tablespoon	grated onion
2 tablespoons	soy sauce
1 teaspoon	ground ginger
1/4 teaspoon	dry mustard
1/8 teaspoon	garlic powder
1 large	green pepper, finely sliced

Season pork chops. In a large skillet, brown chops in oil and remove from heat. Drain all but 2 tablespoons of fat from skillet. Drain peaches, reserving syrup. Blend syrup, sugar, onion, soy sauce, ginger, mustard and garlic powder. Return chops to pan, add syrup mixture, cover and simmer for 30 minutes. Add green pepper and peaches. Simmer for 5 minutes. Serve over rice.

Sautéed String Beans and Pork

Serves 2

1 tablespoon	cornstarch
1 tablespoon	water
1	egg
¼ pound	boneless pork, shredded
½ pound	fresh string beans, French style
4 tablespoons	oil
1 teaspoon	minced garlic
5 — 7	dried chili peppers, minced
1 teaspoon	cooking wine
1 teaspoon	soy sauce
dash	salt
dash	sugar
1 teaspoon	glazing oil (see index)

Combine cornstarch, water and egg; add pork and marinate for 30 minutes. Heat wok* for 10 seconds, add oil and heat for 10 seconds. Add pork and stir for 5 seconds. Add string beans and stir for 10 seconds. Remove. Drain oil from wok. Heat wok for 5 seconds, add garlic and chili peppers. Stir 3 seconds, then add wine, soy sauce, salt and sugar. Return meat and vegetables to wok. Stir quickly for 2 seconds, toss several times, then add Glazing Oil (see index). Toss again and serve immediately.

Howard Co
Yen King
Honolulu, Hawaii

158

Pork Chops Malia

6 (3/4-inch) loin pork chops
              salt and pepper

Dressing

1 (12-ounce) can cream style corn
3/4 cup   finely chopped celery
1 1/4 cups   finely chopped onions
3/4 cup   chopped green pepper
1/4 cup   chopped parsley
1   egg
3 slices   dry bread, broken into small pieces
1/2 teaspoon   thyme

Preheat oven to 350 degrees. Season chops and place in a baking pan. Mix remaining ingredients. Place 1/2 cup of dressing over each chop. Bake for 1 hour.

Cherry Almond Glazed Pork

Serves 8

A colorful, tasty dish for special occasions.

4 pound	pork loin roast; boned, rolled and tied
	salt and pepper
1 (16-ounce) jar	cherry preserves
2 tablespoons	light corn syrup
1/4 cup	red wine vinegar
1/4 teaspoon	ground cinnamon
1/4 teaspoon	ground nutmeg
1/2 teaspoon	ground cloves
1/4 cup	slivered almonds

Preheat oven to 325 degrees. Season roast and bake uncovered in a shallow baking pan for 2 hours. In a saucepan, combine next 6 ingredients and bring to a boil, stirring frequently. Reduce heat and simmer for 2 minutes. Add almonds and keep sauce warm. After roast has cooked for 2 hours, drain off grease, glaze with sauce and return to oven for 30 minutes, basting several times.

Pork Roast
with Plum Sauce

Serves 6—8

3 – 3¹/2-pound   boneless pork roast
salt

Plum Sauce

2 cups	catsup
²/3 cup	sugar
2 tablespoons	hoisin sauce*
2 teaspoons	sesame oil*
¹/2 tablespoon	fresh ginger,* minced
¹/2 tablespoon	salt
2 teaspoons	liquid smoke
2 cloves	garlic, minced
¹/3 cup	cider vinegar

Salt the pork roast and brown in a Dutch oven. Cover and simmer for 1 hour. Pour off fat. Combine sauce ingredients. Add half of the Plum Sauce to pork and continue cooking for 1¹/2 hours. Turn roast periodically. Heat and serve the remaining sauce with the pork.

161

Venison
Steak Molokai

The island of Molokai is noted for its game hunting.

8 (8-ounce)	venison steaks

Marinade

1 cup	olive oil
2 cups	red wine
1 cup	chopped onion
1 cup	sliced carrots
1 cup	chopped celery
4 cloves	garlic, crushed
1 tablespoon	peppercorns
6	bay leaves
8	cloves
1/2 teaspoon	rosemary
1/4 teaspoon	thyme
1/4 teaspoon	oregano

Combine ingredients and marinate venison for 48 hours in the refrigerator, turning occasionally.

Sauce

1/3 cup	clarified butter
1 teaspoon	salt
4 tablespoons	brandy
1 tablespoon	flour
1 teaspoon	beef base
1/2 cup	whipping cream
1/2 cup	sour cream

continued...

Remove steaks from marinade and pat dry. Strain marinade. Sauté 4 steaks at a time in butter. Season with salt. Place all steaks in pan, add brandy and flame. When flame dies, place steaks on a warm platter. Stir flour into pan drippings. Add marinade and beef base and simmer until liquid is reduced by 1/3. Add cream and sour cream. Simmer for 1 to 2 minutes and taste for seasoning. Pour sauce over steaks and serve.

Albert Schmid
Executive Chef
Dillingham Corporation
Honolulu, Hawaii

Broiled Butterflied Leg of Lamb

Serves 8

A subtle blend of flavors complements this lamb dish.

5 – 6 pound	leg of lamb, boned and butterflied
2 cloves	garlic, minced
1/3 cup	lemon juice
1/2 cup	soy sauce
2 tablespoons	thyme
2 tablespoons	Hawaiian rock salt*
	freshly ground pepper
1/2 cup	olive oil

Rub lamb with garlic. Pour lemon juice and soy sauce over the lamb. Sprinkle with thyme, rock salt and pepper. Add oil, coating lamb well. Marinate at room temperature for 4 hours or in the refrigerator 8 to 10 hours. If refrigerated, bring to room temperature before broiling. Broil for 10 to 15 minutes per side for medium-rare lamb. Variation: 2 tablespoons each of tarragon and rosemary may be added to the marinade.

Lamb with Leeks

Serves 6—8

This cooks quickly. Be sure to have all ingredients ready before starting.

3 pound	leg of lamb
3 teaspoons	cornstarch
5 tablespoons	soy sauce
2 teaspoons	Chinese black bean paste*
3 teaspoons	sugar
1 teaspoon	salt
1 teaspoon	pepper
1/2 teaspoon	chili sauce
9 tablespoons	vegetable oil
6 cloves	garlic, minced
1-inch piece	fresh ginger,* thinly sliced
2	leeks, cut into 2-inch lengths and julienned
1 teaspoon	sesame oil*

Cut lamb into thin slices in 1 1/2-inch lengths. Dust lamb with cornstarch. Combine soy sauce, bean paste, sugar, salt, pepper and chili sauce. Add lamb to sauce. Heat 6 tablespoons vegetable oil in a large skillet. Add garlic and ginger and stir-fry for 30 seconds. Add lamb and stir-fry for 3 minutes or until lamb is no longer pink. Remove from heat, drain and set aside. Add remaining vegetable oil and leeks and stir-fry until wilted. Add lamb and sesame oil and stir-fry for 1 1/2 minutes. Serve immediately.

Chicken Macadamia *Serves 8–10*

2 – 2¹/₂ pounds   boneless chicken breasts, skinned

Batter

2	eggs
¹/₂ cup	flour
¹/₄ cup	cornstarch
1 tablespoon	finely chopped fresh ginger*
1 medium	onion, grated
¹/₂ teaspoon	black pepper
2 tablespoons	peanut oil
2 tablespoons	brandy
2 tablespoons	soy sauce
	salt to taste
	peanut oil

Sauce

6 tablespoons	brown sugar
3 tablespoons	soy sauce
1¹/₂ tablespoons	cornstarch
¹/₂ cup	vinegar
³/₄ cup	cold water
	*Garnish: Chopped macadamia nuts**

Cut each chicken breast in 6 pieces. Mix the batter ingredients in a blender. Marinate the chicken pieces in the batter for 20 minutes. Meanwhile, combine the sauce ingredients and simmer over low heat for 15 minutes. Deep fry the chicken pieces in peanut oil at 350 degrees for 8 to 10 minutes or until done. Drain. Place the chicken over rice. Spoon on the sauce and top with macadamia nuts. Variation: Try this with Fried Rice (see index).

Kun Pao Chicken   *Serves 4*

Kun Pao literally means "chili pepper spicy hot" in Mandarin.

1 tablespoon	water
1	egg, beaten
1 tablespoon	cornstarch
1/2 pound	boneless chicken, cut into 1-inch cubes
6 cups	vegetable oil
1 (8-ounce) can	water chestnuts,* diced
2	green onion tops, cut into 1-inch lengths
2 ounces	unsalted roasted peanuts
1 clove	garlic, minced
5	Hawaiian chili peppers,* chopped
1/4 teaspoon	minced fresh ginger *
1 teaspoon	wine
1 teaspoon	soy sauce
dash	salt
1/2 teaspoon	sugar
1 tablespoon	chicken broth
1 teaspoon	Glazing Oil (see index)

Combine water, egg and cornstarch to make batter. Add chicken. Stir vigorously, then let stand 30 minutes. Heat wok* for 10 seconds, then add vegetable oil. Heat oil, add chicken and stir to separate chicken cubes. Add water chestnuts, onion and peanuts. Stir for 5 seconds and drain. Heat wok for 5 seconds, add garlic, chili peppers and ginger. Stir quickly, then add wine and soy sauce. Toss several times, then add salt, sugar and broth. Simmer for 5 seconds and add cornstarch solution to thicken. Add glazing oil, toss and transfer to serving platter.

Howard Co
Yen King
Honolulu, Hawaii

Lemon Chicken

A Chinese favorite.

3 pounds	boneless chicken breasts
1 tablespoon	sherry
1 tablespoon	soy sauce
1/2 teaspoon	salt
2	eggs
1/4 cup	cornstarch
1/2 teaspoon	baking powder
2 cups	vegetable oil
1/3 cup	sugar
1 tablespoon	cornstarch
1 cup	chicken broth
1 tablespoon	lemon juice
1 teaspoon	salt
2 tablespoons	vegetable oil
1	lemon, thinly sliced

Combine chicken with sherry, soy sauce and salt. Marinate for 15 minutes. Beat eggs, cornstarch and baking powder to form a smooth batter. Heat oil to 350 degrees. Coat chicken with batter and fry until brown. Cut into 1 by 1 1/2-inch pieces and arrange on a serving dish. Combine sugar, 1 tablespoon cornstarch, broth, lemon juice and salt. Heat remaining oil. Stir-fry the lemon slices for 30 seconds. Slowly stir in cornstarch mixture. Cook, stirring constantly, until sauce is clear. Pour over chicken and serve immediately.

Miso Chicken

Serves 10

Chicken fillets done in the Japanese style.

6 pounds	boneless chicken breasts
1/2 cup	prepared red miso*
or	
1/2 cup	white miso* with 1/2 teaspoon sugar and 2 teaspoons mirin*
3 stalks	green onion, sliced diagonally
1 1/2 teaspoons	toasted sesame seeds
1/4 cup	shredded pickled red ginger*

Marinate the chicken in the miso for 1/2 hour. Broil chicken on both sides for 3 minutes, being careful not to overcook. Slice chicken and top with onion, sesame seeds and ginger.

Chinese
Minute Chicken

Serves 6 — 8

3 pounds	chicken thighs, boned and cubed
3 – 5 tablespoons	cornstarch
1/4 cup	vegetable oil
1 tablespoon	sesame oil*
2 cloves	garlic, minced
1 teaspoon	minced fresh ginger*
1/4 teaspoon	salt
1/4 teaspoon	pepper
2 tablespoons	sherry
1/2 cup	water
1 tablespoon	cornstarch
1 1/2 tablespoons	brown sugar
1/2 cup	oyster sauce*
1/2 cup	chopped green onions
1/2 cup	chopped Chinese parsley*
	lettuce leaves

Coat chicken with cornstarch. Heat oils and sauté garlic and ginger until browned. Stir-fry chicken on high heat, sprinkling with salt, pepper and sherry, until chicken is browned. Reduce heat to medium. Dissolve cornstarch in water. Add sugar and oyster sauce, combining well. Pour over chicken. Add green onions and parsley. Serve on lettuce leaves.

Chicken with Peppers and Pecans

Serves 4

A surprising taste treat.

2 teaspoons	cornstarch
3 tablespoons	soy sauce
2 tablespoons	sherry or mirin*
1 teaspoon	grated fresh ginger*
1 teaspoon	sugar
1/2 teaspoon	salt
2 tablespoons	vegetable oil
2 medium	green peppers, cut into 3/4-inch strips
4	green onions, diagonally sliced in 1-inch lengths
1 cup	pecan halves
1 1/2 pounds	whole chicken breasts, skinned, boned and cubed

In a small bowl, dissolve cornstarch in soy sauce. Add sherry, ginger, sugar and salt. Heat oil in wok* and stir-fry green peppers and onions for 2 minutes. Remove from wok. Stir-fry pecans for 1 to 2 minutes. Remove. Add more oil if necessary. Stir-fry half the chicken until done and remove. Repeat with remaining chicken. Return all chicken to wok. Add soy sauce mixture and stir until thickened. Add vegetables and nuts. Cover wok and cook for 1 minute. Variation: For color, drained Mandarin oranges may be added with vegetables and nuts.

Evil Jungle Prince

Serves 2

3 – 4 tablespoons	dried red curry stock*
1/4 cup	vegetable oil
1/2 cup	coconut milk*
1/2 pound	sliced boneless chicken breast, skinned
10 – 15	fresh basil leaves
4 tablespoons	Thai fish sauce*
1/2 cup	chopped white cabbage

Sauté the dried red curry stock in heated vegetable oil for 3 minutes. Add coconut milk and cook for 2 minutes on medium heat. Add chicken. Cook for 5 minutes. Lower heat to medium low, add basil and fish sauce and serve on a bed of chopped cabbage. Note: Coconut milk will separate if allowed to come to a boil.

Keo Sananikone
Keo's
Honolulu, Hawaii

Steamed Chicken with Lup Cheong

Serves 6

6 – 7	dried black Chinese mushrooms*
1¹/2 teaspoons	sugar
3 tablespoons	soy sauce
2 tablespoons	water
2 – 3	Lup Cheong sausages,* cut diagonally
3 pounds	boneless chicken, skinned and cut in 1-inch pieces
1 tablespoon	hoisin sauce*
2 cloves	garlic, minced
1 tablespoon	bourbon
1 tablespoon	chopped green onion
1 tablespoon	minced fresh ginger*
1¹/2 tablespoons	cornstarch

Garnish: Chopped green onion

Soak mushrooms in warm water for 20 minutes. Drain and remove tough stems. Slice into strips. In a skillet, combine sugar, soy sauce and water. Add sausages and simmer for 10 minutes. In a bowl, combine remaining ingredients. Add simmered mixture and marinate for ¹/2 hour. Steam,* covered, for ¹/2 hour or until done. Garnish.

Thai Chicken Curry

Mint leaves and zucchini enhance this Thai curry.

3 pounds	boneless chicken breasts, skinned and cubed
2 tablespoons	cornstarch
1/4 cup	butter
1 medium	onion, diced
1 clove	garlic, minced
1 tablespoon	curry powder
1 tablespoon	minced fresh ginger*
1 (12-ounce) can	frozen coconut milk,* thawed
1 tablespoon	Thai fish sauce*
2 small	zucchini, diced
1/2 cup	mint leaves
4	green onions, thinly sliced
1 teaspoon	crushed red pepper
	salt and pepper to taste

Coat chicken with cornstarch. In a large skillet or wok,* sauté onions and garlic until soft. Add chicken, curry powder and ginger and stir-fry for 2 minutes. Add coconut milk, fish sauce and zucchini and simmer for 3 minutes. Add remaining ingredients and simmer for one minute. Serve over rice.

173

Mom's Chicken Curry $\qquad$ *Serves 8 – 10*

The recipe can be used with beef, lamb, shellfish, tuna or a combination of fresh vegetables.

1/2 cup	butter
4 tablespoons	chopped onions
2 cloves	garlic, minced
4 tablespoons	curry powder
6 tablespoons	flour
8	chicken bouillon cubes
4 cups	water
1	apple, pared and chopped
5 – 6 cups	cooked chicken, cubed
1 pint	whipping cream

In melted butter, sauté onions and garlic with curry powder for 5 minutes. Add flour and stir until smooth. Combine bouillon and water and slowly add to flour mixture. Stir until thoroughly blended. Add apple and chicken and simmer, covered, for 1 hour. Add cream. Heat thoroughly without boiling. Serve with fluffy white rice and 6 to 8 condiments from the following list.

Curry Condiments

Chopped bananas	Diced avocado
Chutney	Chopped green pepper
Grated egg	Diced tomatoes
Chopped green onions	Green or ripe olives
Coconut, shredded or toasted	Plain yogurt
Raisins	Chopped nuts
Chopped bacon	Chopped cucumbers

Chicken Curry Crêpes   *Serves 8*

Especially good with the Mandarin Almond Salad.

3 tablespoons	butter, melted
1 cup	finely chopped onion
2 teaspoons	chopped parsley
3 tablespoons	flour
$1^{1}/_{2}$ – 2 tablespoons	curry powder
2 cups	chicken broth
$1^{1}/_{2}$ cups	whipping cream
2 tablespoons	shredded coconut
	salt and pepper to taste
4 cups	cooked and cubed chicken breasts
$^{3}/_{4}$ cup	golden seedless raisins
16	crêpes (see index)
$^{1}/_{3}$ cup	chopped peanuts

Sauté onion and parsley in butter until onion is soft but not brown. Stir in flour and curry powder and cook for one minute. Gradually stir in chicken broth and cream. When smooth, add coconut and simmer for five minutes. Add half the curry sauce to the chicken and raisins. Place 2 to 3 tablespoons of chicken mixture on each crêpe. Roll the crêpes and place seam side down in a buttered baking dish. Cover with remaining curry sauce. Crêpes may be refrigerated at this point for several hours or baked in preheated 350 degree oven for 30 minutes or until sauce bubbles. Sprinkle with nuts and bake for five minutes. Garnish with Curry Condiments.

Wiki Wiki
Chicken in a Bag
Serves 4 – 6

"Wiki Wiki" means "quick" in Hawaiian.
An easy way to fix chicken for those recipes calling for cooked chicken.

1 – 2	whole chicken fryers
	vegetable cooking spray
2 large	brown grocery bags, doubled for extra thickness

Preheat oven to 450 degrees. Remove giblets from chicken cavity. Rinse chicken and pat dry. Spray inside of grocery bag with vegetable cooking spray. Place chickens in bag and fold down to close. Place the bag on a rimmed cookie sheet and bake for 1^{1}/$_{2}$ hours. Note: In order to preserve the juices do not be tempted to salt the chicken. Do not use recycled paper bags.

Barbara's Chicken
Serves 6 – 8

4 pounds	boneless chicken breasts
^{1}/$_{4}$ cup	butter
	salt, pepper and paprika
2 (10^{3}/$_{4}$-ounce) cans	cream of chicken soup
^{1}/$_{2}$ pound	fresh mushrooms, sliced
1 (8-ounce) can	water chestnuts,* sliced
^{1}/$_{2}$ cup	white wine
^{1}/$_{2}$ cup	sliced almonds

Preheat oven to 350 degrees. Place chicken in a 9 x 13-inch baking dish. Dot with butter and season. Bake for 45 minutes. Mix soup, mushrooms, water chestnuts and wine. Pour over chicken. Sprinkle almonds on top and bake uncovered in 300 degree oven for 30 minutes.

Chicken Liz

Serves 10

1/3 cup	butter
4 pounds	boneless chicken breasts, skinned and cut in large bite-size pieces
1 cup	chopped onion
1 clove	garlic, minced
2 teaspoons	salt
1 tablespoon	ground ginger
1/4 teaspoon	chili powder
1/2 – 1 cup	canned tomatoes, drained
1 cup	plain yogurt
1/2 cup	chopped macadamia nuts* or cashews
1/2 cup	flaked coconut
1/2 cup	raisins
2 tablespoons	cornstarch
1 cup	whipping cream

Melt butter and brown chicken in a Dutch oven. Remove chicken and set aside. Sauté onion and garlic in remaining butter for 5 minutes. Add salt, ginger, chili, tomatoes, yogurt and chicken. Cover and cook for 15 minutes. Stir in nuts, coconut and raisins. Cover and simmer for 10 minutes until chicken is tender. Dissolve cornstarch in cream and add to chicken. Stir constantly, heating sauce thoroughly for 5 minutes. Serve with noodles or brown rice and Lime Baked Papaya (see index).

Coconut Chicken with Fresh Fruit

Serves 4 — 6

Delightful blend of flavors.

1/3 cup	flaked coconut
2 tablespoons	butter
8 large	boneless chicken breasts, skinned
1 tablespoon	finely chopped fresh ginger,*
or	
3/4 teaspoon	ground ginger
1/2 teaspoon	salt
1 cup	whipping cream
3 large	firm, ripe bananas, quartered
1 large	ripe papaya,* peeled, seeded, halved and sliced
	Garnish: Lime wedges

Toast coconut in 300 degree oven for 10 minutes. Set aside. In a large frying pan, brown chicken breasts in butter. Sprinkle ginger, 3 tablespoons coconut and salt over chicken. Add cream, cover and cook over medium heat for 10 minutes or until done. Remove chicken and arrange with fruit on a large platter. Spoon sauce over chicken and sprinkle with remaining toasted coconut. Garnish with limes to be squeezed over chicken and fruit.

Herb Chicken

Serves 6—8

An excellent picnic choice which may be served hot or cold.

3 – 4 pounds	chicken parts, skinned
1/2 tablespoon	tarragon
1/2 tablespoon	basil
1/2 tablespoon	thyme
1/2 tablespoon	garlic salt
1/2 tablespoon	freshly ground pepper
1 tablespoon	seasoned salt
3 tablespoons	olive oil
1 large	lemon, thinly sliced
	juice of 1 lemon
2	bay leaves

Preheat oven to 350 degrees. Combine seasonings and sprinkle over chicken. Cover the bottom of a baking dish with olive oil. Add chicken and cover with lemon slices. Drizzle lemon juice over chicken, add bay leaves and bake for 30 minutes. Turn chicken and bake for 15 to 20 minutes. Remove bay leaves. Serve hot or cold. Remove lemon slices before refrigerating.

Chicken Aspic

Elegant for a very special luncheon or light summer dinner.

1¹/₂ pounds	chicken breasts
1 teaspoon	salt
2 (14-ounce) cans	chicken broth
6 envelopes	unflavored gelatin
6	green onions, chopped
2 cups	chopped celery and leaves
1 cup	chopped Maui onion*
1 (7-ounce) can	sliced pimientos
1 teaspoon	coarse ground black pepper
¹/₂ cup	sliced stuffed olives
	watercress

Skin and poach chicken breasts in salted broth until tender, approximately 15 minutes. Remove chicken, shred and set aside. Add gelatin to broth and cool. Place vegetables in loaf pan with pimientos, pepper, olives and chicken. Pour broth over ingredients and refrigerate until set. Turn out on a bed of fresh watercress and serve with Sauce Albert (see index).

Albert Schmid
Executive Chef
Dillingham Corporation
Honolulu, Hawaii

Chicken Tarragon   *Serves 4 — 6*

3¹/2 – 4 pounds	boneless chicken breasts, skinned
4 tablespoons	melted butter
	salt and white pepper
¹/2 cup	dry white wine
3 – 4 tablespoons	Pernod or Anisette
1 tablespoon	tarragon leaves
1 cup	whipping cream, slightly whipped
1 tablespoon	arrowroot
¹/2 teaspoon	salt
¹/4 teaspoon	white pepper

Garnish: Chopped parsley

Preheat oven to 350 degrees. Brush butter over chicken breasts. Sprinkle with salt and pepper. Bake, partially covered, for 30 minutes or until just tender. Transfer chicken to a plate and keep warm. Add to the pan juices the wine, Pernod and tarragon and bring to a boil. Lower heat and stir in cream, arrowroot dissolved in a little cream to make a paste, salt and pepper. Blend well and simmer until slightly thickened. Pour sauce over chicken and garnish with parsley.

Chicken Simon and Garfunkel

Serves 6—8

Seasoned with parsley, sage, rosemary and thyme, of course!

3¹/₂ – 4 pounds	boneless chicken breasts, skinned
¹/₄ – ¹/₂ cup	butter, softened
	salt and pepper
8 (3 x 5-inch) slices	Mozzarella cheese
1	egg, beaten
2 tablespoons	water
	flour
	bread crumbs
¹/₂ cup	melted butter
1 tablespoon	parsley
¹/₄ teaspoon	sage
¹/₄ teaspoon	rosemary
¹/₄ teaspoon	thyme
¹/₂ cup	sherry

Preheat oven to 350 degrees. Pound each chicken breast until thin. Brush liberally with butter. Season with salt and pepper. Lay each chicken breast on a slice of cheese and roll up, fastening with a toothpick. Combine the beaten egg with water. Roll the chicken in the flour, egg mixture and crumbs. Evenly space in a baking pan. Combine the melted butter with parsley, sage, rosemary and thyme. Drizzle the herbed butter over the chicken rolls. Bake for 30 minutes. Pour the sherry over the chicken and bake an additional 30 minutes. Note: The cheese will soften but not melt, so don't worry about rolling chicken in cheese.

Pineapple Duck
Serves 4

Crispy roast duck with a tart sweet sour sauce.

4 – 5 pound	duck, quartered
1 tablespoon	salt
2 tablespoons	honey
3 tablespoons	soy sauce
1 teaspoon	grated orange peel
1/2 cup	orange juice
1/4 cup	wine vinegar
1/2 teaspoon	onion powder
1 cup	pineapple chunks, drained
2 teaspoons	cornstarch
3 tablespoons	cold water

Preheat oven to 450 degrees. Remove any visible fat from duck and sprinkle with salt. Roast for 30 minutes. Combine honey, soy sauce, orange peel, juice, vinegar and onion powder. Transfer duck to shallow baking pan. Coat with half of the sauce and bake for an additional 45 minutes. Baste frequently. Add pineapple to remainder of sauce and heat. Combine cornstarch with water and stir into the sauce. Bring to a boil and serve with duck.

Baked Kumu   *Serves 4*

2 pounds	whole kumu,* red snapper or sea bass
	salt and pepper
1 tablespoon	fresh lemon juice
	dried fennel leaves (optional)
1/2 cup	butter
1/2 – 1 cup	thinly sliced onion
3 tablespoons	butter
2 medium	potatoes, peeled and thinly sliced
2 medium	tomatoes, quartered
1/2 cup	white wine
3 tablespoons	Pernod
	Garnish: Chopped parsley and 1 lemon, quartered

Preheat oven to 375 degrees. Season fish inside and out with salt, pepper and lemon juice. Place fennel leaves inside fish. Melt butter and brown fish on both sides. Place fish and remaining butter in baking dish and bake for 10 minutes. Sauté onion in 3 tablespoons butter and place around the fish, baking an additional 10 minutes. Parboil the potatoes in salted water. Add potatoes to the fish and bake for an additional 20 minutes. Add tomatoes and pour the wine over the fish. Sprinkle with Pernod. Bake for 8 minutes. Place fish on a serving platter. Arrange vegetables around the fish. Pour juices from the baking dish over the fish and garnish.

Maile Restaurant
Kahala Hilton
Honolulu, Hawaii

Moragné Fillets

Serves 2

A quick and easy dish.

1 pound	fresh fish fillets, ahi* or mahimahi*
	juice of 1 lemon
1/2 cup	flour
4 tablespoons	butter
3/4 cup	whipping cream

Marinate fish in lemon juice for 10 to 30 minutes. Roll in flour and sauté in butter until firm. Transfer fish to warm platter. Cover and keep warm. Add cream to pan drippings along with any remaining lemon juice and flour. Heat, stirring until smooth. Pour over fish and serve.

Panko Ulua Fillet

Fried fish with a nice crispy coating.

Ulua* fillet or Papio* fillet
pepper
mayonnaise
panko*
vegetable oil

Season fish, spread generously with mayonnaise and bread with panko. Pan fry on low heat until golden brown using 1/8-inch vegetable oil in pan. Do not overcook.

Hari Kojima
Let's Go Fishing
Channel 2
Honolulu, Hawaii

Mahimahi with Leek

Serves 6—8

2¹/2 pounds	mahimahi* fillets
1 cup	flour
4	eggs, beaten
¹/2 cup	butter
1 cup	vegetable oil
3	shallots, minced
2 cloves	garlic, minced
1	leek, julienned
1 teaspoon	salt
¹/2 teaspoon	pepper
2 tablespoons	lemon juice
1 cup	fish stock

Garnish: Parsley and lemon wedges

Cut mahimahi into 3-ounce medallions. Dip in flour, then beaten eggs and sauté for 2¹/2 minutes on each side in all but one tablespoon each of butter and oil. Arrange medallions on serving tray. Heat reserved butter and oil in a skillet, glaze shallots and garlic. Add leeks and sauté mixture for 3 minutes. Season with salt, pepper and lemon juice. Deglaze with fish stock. Spoon sauce over fish. Garnish and serve.

Chef Kim Dietrich
Mauna Kea Beach Hotel
Kamuela, Hawaii

Plaza Club Mahimahi

1/2 cup	mayonnaise
2 tablespoons	lemon juice
2 ounces	crabmeat
1/4 cup	finely diced celery
3/4 pound	avocado, finely diced
dash	Worcestershire sauce
	salt and pepper to taste
4 (5-ounce)	mahimahi* fillets

Preheat oven to 350 degrees. Combine mayonnaise, lemon juice, crabmeat, celery and avocado. Season with Worcestershire, salt and pepper. Place fillets in a lightly buttered baking pan and spread evenly with avocado mixture. Do not let the thickness of the mixture exceed 1/2 inch. Bake for 10 to 15 minutes.

Russell Siu
Plaza Club
Honolulu, Hawaii

Chinese Steamed Salmon

Serves 4

2 pounds   salmon steaks
            salt
1/2 cup   butter
3 cloves   garlic, minced
           *Garnish: Chinese parsley**

Salt the salmon steaks and place on paper towels for 15 minutes. Arrange salmon in a large bowl. Dot salmon with butter and sprinkle with garlic. Place bowl in a steamer and steam* covered for 10 to 15 minutes. Garnish and serve.

Fish Divine

Serves 4

4   firm white fish fillets (see fish chart)
    salt and pepper
3   firm bananas
    lemon juice
1/2   ripe papaya,* peeled and seeded
1/2 cup   melted butter
2 tablespoons   lemon juice

Arrange fish in a single layer in a buttered dish. Sprinkle with salt and pepper. Cut bananas in 1/2 inch diagonal slices and dip in lemon juice. Cut papaya into slices. Arrange fruit around fish. Pour 1/4 cup butter over fish and fruit. Broil 3 inches from the heat for 5 minutes. Add lemon juice to remaining butter. Pour over fish and fruit. Serve.

Steamed Fish— Chinese Style

1 – 2 pounds	fresh whole white fish (see fish chart)
1 teaspoon	sugar
1 teaspoon	salt
2 tablespoons	sherry
2 tablespoons	soy sauce
1 tablespoon	vegetable oil
1	onion, sliced
1 tablespoon	chopped fresh ginger*
1 tablespoon	Chinese black beans*
1 clove	garlic, minced
8 ounces	Lup Cheong,* sliced
1 bunch	Chinese parsley*

Clean fish. Combine sugar, salt, sherry and soy sauce. Rub fish with marinade, inside and out. Let sit 20 minutes to 1 hour. Place fish in shallow bowl. Cover with oil, onion, ginger, black beans, garlic, Lup Cheong and Chinese parsley. (May stuff cavity with same.) Steam* for 20 minutes or until fish flakes.

Fillet of Sole
with Lychee

Serves 4 — 6

Poaching Liquid

1^1/$_2$ – 2 cups	chicken or fish stock
^{1}/$_2$ – ^{3}/$_4$ cup	white wine
2	shallots, minced
3	green onion tops, chopped
dash	white pepper

Bring ingredients to a boil in a flat sauté pan or metal gratin pan.

Fish

8	sole fillets or opakapaka*
16	seedless grapes
16	lychee,* canned or fresh (pitted and peeled)
3 tablespoons	butter

Break line on fillets by tapping lightly with knife to facilitate rolling. Cut down spine, dividing in two. Place rough side up and salt lightly. Stuff lychee with seedless grapes and roll one in each strip of sole. Secure with toothpicks. Turn heat off poaching liquid and place rolls in the liquid. Add 2 tablespoons butter and cover with 10 x 14-inch sheet of brown paper bag (not recycled) which has been heavily buttered with 1 tablespoon butter. Place buttered side over fish and bake on lowest rack in oven for 7 to 10 minutes at 475 degrees. Remove from oven and place in ovenproof serving dish. Cover and set aside.

continued...

Velouté Sauce

	reduced poaching liquid
1¹/2 cups	Half and Half
1 tablespoon	butter
1 tablespoon	flour
	freshly grated nutmeg
dash	white pepper
	salt to taste
¹/4 – ¹/3 cup	grated Swiss cheese
	juice of ¹/2 lemon

Garnish: Minced parsley

Strain poaching liquid into a saucepan and boil down to half (6 to 7 minutes). Heat Half and Half to near boil. Make a roux in a 1-quart saucepan by melting butter and stirring in flour. Cook at medium heat for 1 minute. Do not brown. Remove roux from heat and stir in hot Half and Half and mix vigorously with a wire whisk. Add half of the reduced poaching liquid, nutmeg, white pepper and salt. Bring to a slow boil and add Swiss cheese, stirring constantly with a whisk. Add lemon juice. Pour the sauce evenly over the poached sole rolls and place under the broiler for 2 to 3 minutes or until the sauce is bubbling. Allow to stay until it begins to turn a slightly golden color in places. Garnish and serve.

Nino J. Martin
The International Chef Ⓡ
Hawaii Public Television
Honolulu, Hawaii

Red Snapper Fillets in Artichoke Butter

Serves 6

An exciting mixture of vegetables and seafood.

6	red snapper fillets (2 – 2^1/2 pounds)
^{1}/2 cup	butter
4 tablespoons	green onion tops, chopped
2 tablespoons	parsley, chopped
3 cloves	garlic, minced
1 tablespoon	lemon juice
1 (8-ounce) can	sliced mushrooms, drained
1 (14-ounce) can	artichoke hearts, drained and sliced
1 teaspoon	salt
^{1}/2 teaspoon	cayenne pepper

Pat fillets dry with paper towels and place in a flat baking dish. In a 4-cup measuring cup, sauté butter, onion tops, parsley and garlic using microwave oven on high for 2 minutes. Add lemon juice, mushrooms, artichokes, salt and cayenne. Microwave on high 2 minutes or until mixture is heated through. Pour sauce over fish. Cover with wax paper and cook on high 7 to 8 minutes or until fish flakes easily with a fork. Let stand covered 3 minutes. Note: Allow 3 minutes cooking time per pound of fish at room temperature.

Jean K Durkee
Tout de Suite à la Microwave

Stuffed Opakapaka

Serves 4 – 6

3 – 6 pound	fresh opakapaka*
1/2 teaspoon	garlic salt
1/4 teaspoon	black pepper
	vegetable oil
1 – 2 cloves	garlic, minced
8 ounces	scallops, sliced
8 ounces	crab meat
1	onion, diced
8 – 12 ounces	fresh mushrooms, sliced
1/4 cup	white wine (optional)
1 1/3 cups	mayonnaise
	paprika

Preheat oven to 375 degrees. Clean fish and cut butterfly style. Season with garlic salt and pepper. Set aside. In a frying pan or large saucepan, brown garlic in a small amount of vegetable oil. Add scallops, crabmeat, onion and mushrooms. Just before mushrooms are fully cooked add wine. Continue cooking for 1 to 2 minutes. Remove from heat. Place mixture in a large mixing bowl, retaining a minimum of liquid. Mix thoroughly with mayonnaise. Place fish in a lightly greased baking pan. Fill cavity with mixture. Sprinkle with paprika and bake uncovered for 30 to 35 minutes.

Hari Kojima
Let's Go Fishing
Channel 2
Honolulu, Hawaii

Opakapaka with Shrimp and Almonds

Serves 1

7 ounce	opakapaka* fillet
4 ounces	clarified butter, melted
2 ounces	clam juice
	juice of 1/2 lemon
1/2 teaspoon	seasoning salt

Shrimp and Almond Sauce

2 – 3	shrimp
1/4 cup	almonds, sliced or slivered
2 – 3 tablespoons	butter
dash	seasoning salt
1/2 ounce	white wine

Garnish: Chopped parsley

Preheat oven to 375 degrees. Place fish and remaining ingredients in an ovenproof baking dish and bake for 10 minutes. In a separate skillet, sauté shrimp and almonds in butter. Add salt and wine. Place fish on the plate. Top with shrimp and almonds. Lace the sauce over the fish and garnish with chopped parsley.

Alfred "Almar" Arcano
Executive Chef
Hy's Steak House
Honolulu, Hawaii

Kona Inn Onaga

Serves 1 — 2

Can be prepared in advance and refrigerated until ready to bake.

8 ounces	onaga,* deboned
	flour
2 tablespoons	butter
3 ounces	green chili salsa
2 ounces	Monterey Jack cheese, shredded
1 ounce	Cheddar cheese, shredded
	salt and pepper
	Garnish: Chopped parsley

Preheat oven to 350 degrees. Lightly flour fish and sauté in butter for approximately one minute on each side to seal in juices. Put fish in casserole and top with salsa. Sprinkle Cheddar cheese on center of fish and Monterey Jack on each end. Bake for 10 to 12 minutes. Garnish with chopped parsley.

Kona Inn Restaurant
Kailua-Kona, Hawaii

Crabmeat Baked in Avocado

Serves 8

4 (1-pound)	ripe avocados
4 cloves	garlic, crushed
	juice of 2 lemons
3 pints	Newburg Sauce (see index)
2 pounds	crabmeat
1/2 cup	chopped celery
1/4 cup	chopped green onion
5	egg whites, stiffly beaten
	grated Parmesan cheese
	bread crumbs
1/4 cup	melted butter

Preheat oven to 350 degrees. Cut avocado in half lengthwise and discard seed. Score the inside and add crushed garlic and lemon juice. Let stand for 1/2 hour, then discard juice and garlic. Set aside. Drain and squeeze excess moisture from crabmeat. Add celery, green onion and Newburg Sauce. Fold in egg whites. Fill avocados with crabmeat mixture. Sprinkle with bread crumbs and Parmesan cheese and dribble melted butter on top. Bake for 25 minutes.

Albert Schmid
Executive Chef
Dillingham Corporation
Honolulu, Hawaii

Crabmeat Stir-Fry *Serves 4*

All ingredients must be ready to cook because the cooking is very quick and timing is essential.

6 – 8	green onions, chopped (including tops)
2 tablespoons	vegetable oil
5 tablespoons	butter
1 large	green pepper, chopped
1/2 pound	mushrooms, sliced
1 cup	sliced water chestnuts*
3 cups	cooked rice
1 pound	crabmeat
1/4 cup	chopped parsley
	salt and pepper to taste

Sauté green onions in oil and butter for 2 minutes. Stir in green pepper and mushrooms and cook for 2 minutes. Add water chestnuts, rice and crabmeat. Stir-fry until thoroughly heated. Add seasonings and serve immediately.

Crab Enchiladas

Well worth the effort.

Salsa con Tomatillos

2 (10-ounce) cans	tomatillos, drained, reserve liquid
1/4 cup	vegetable oil
2	corn tortillas
1/4 cup	vegetable oil
2	fresh jalapeño chilies, seeded and chopped or 2 (3-ounce) cans chopped chilies (for milder taste)
1/2 cup	chopped onion
1 clove	garlic
1 teaspoon	salt
1/2 teaspoon	cumin
1 teaspoon	cilantro*
dash	sugar

Fry tortillas in oil, browning lightly. Crumble fried tortillas into tomatillos liquid and let soften. Blend or process mixture and tomatillos until smooth. Sauté chilies and onions in 1/4 cup oil until onion is soft. Crush garlic with salt, cumin and cilantro and add to chilies and onions. Cook for 5 minutes. Add blended tortilla mixture and cook for 5 minutes. Set aside.

continued...

Sour Cream Sauce

1 clove	garlic
1/2 teaspoon	salt
1/2 pint	sour cream
2 tablespoons	chopped onion
dash	sugar

Thoroughly mash garlic in salt. Add sour cream, onion and sugar, mixing well. Refrigerate.

Enchiladas

1 1/2 cups	crabmeat
	butter
6	corn tortillas
2 – 3 tablespoons	vegetable oil
6 tablespoons	minced onion
8 – 10 ounces	Jack cheese, shredded
	Salsa con Tomatillos
	Sour Cream Sauce

Garnish: Pitted black olives, sliced avocado and sliced tomato

Preheat oven to 400 degrees. Sauté crabmeat in butter. Fry tortillas in oil until soft. Place 1/4 cup crabmeat in center of each tortilla. Sprinkle with 1 tablespoon onion and spoon one tablespoon of Salsa con Tomatillos on each. Roll each tortilla (now called an enchilada) and place seam side down in a shallow baking dish. Cover with remaining salsa. Sprinkle generously with cheese and bake for 10 minutes or until cheese is melted. Serve with a dollop of Sour Cream Sauce and garnish.

Westport Shrimp

Serves 6—8

A rich baked casserole with a hint of curry.

1/2 cup	butter
2 cups	whipping cream
2 tablespoons	cornstarch
1 teaspoon	curry powder
3 ounces	sherry
3 cups	cooked medium shrimp
or	
5 cups	cooked diced chicken
2 cups	cooked rice
1/2 – 3/4 cup	golden raisins (optional)
	garlic salt and lemon pepper to taste
3/4 cup	grated Swiss cheese

Preheat oven to 325 degrees. Grease a 3-quart casserole. In a saucepan, bring butter and cream to a boil. Reduce heat. Mix cornstarch and curry with the sherry and add to the cream. Cook until thickened, stirring constantly. Add shrimp or chicken, rice and raisins. Blend in seasonings and pour mixture into casserole. Sprinkle cheese over the top and bake uncovered for 30 minutes or until cheese is melted and slightly browned.

Broccoli
Speared Shrimp

1¹/2 pounds	fresh broccoli
1 teaspoon	salt
26	medium shrimp, shelled and deveined
2	egg whites
1 teaspoon	cornstarch
4 – 8 tablespoons	vegetable oil
6 cloves	garlic, minced
	salt and pepper

Trim broccoli, cut lengthwise into 26 spears about 4 inches long. Pare ends of broccoli to a point. Blanch broccoli in boiling salted water for 45 seconds. Remove from heat, drain and add cool water to stop cooking process. Broccoli should be firm. Drain and set aside. Make a small slit in back of each shrimp. (Slit must be small or shrimp will slip off broccoli during cooking.) Whip egg whites slightly and mix in cornstarch. Add shrimp. Spear broccoli through slit in shrimp. Heat 4 tablespoons of oil in a skillet, add garlic and cook over high heat. Add 6 to 8 shrimp spears and toss quickly. Remove when shrimp turns pink. Repeat, adding more oil as needed. Season with salt and pepper. Note: This could also be used as a pupu.*

The Willows
Shrimp Curry

Serves 6

Curry Sauce

6 tablespoons	clarified butter
3 cloves	garlic, minced
1/4 cup	chopped fresh ginger*
2 cups	finely chopped onions
3 teaspoons	salt
3 teaspoons	sugar
3 tablespoons	curry powder
9 tablespoons	flour
2 quarts	coconut milk*

Sauté garlic, ginger and onion in clarified butter. Add salt, sugar, curry powder and flour. Mix thoroughly. Add coconut milk a little at a time, stirring to a smooth thickness and cook for 20 minutes until sauce begins to boil. Allow to stand several hours. Strain before using.

2 pounds	shrimp (preferably 21 – 25 count per pound)
6 ounces	white wine or dry vermouth
3 tablespoons	peanut oil
	salt and pepper to taste
6 tablespoons	curry powder

Peel shrimp. Cut lengthwise in half. Devein and wash. Marinate shrimp in white wine or dry vermouth and peanut oil. Add pinch of salt and pepper. Let stand 15 minutes. Pan fry curry powder in saucepan. Add marinated shrimp. When shrimp turns pink, pour in curry sauce. Note: Chicken is prepared in same manner.

The Willows
Honolulu, Hawaii

Seafood à la Crème

A favorite dish for gourmands prior to running in the annual Honolulu Marathon.

12 ounces	green spinach noodles
3 tablespoons	butter
2 medium	onions, finely chopped
1 pound	fresh mushrooms, sliced
1^1/2 pounds	crab, shrimp or lobster,
	cut in bite-size pieces
2 cups	sour cream
^{3}/4 cup	dry white wine
2 teaspoons	Worcestershire sauce
2 (10^3/4-ounce) cans	cream of mushroom soup
2 tablespoons	flour
2 tablespoons	curry powder
1^1/2 cups	grated sharp Cheddar cheese
1 teaspoon	oregano
^{1}/2 teaspoon	paprika

Preheat oven to 350 degrees. Cook spinach noodles and drain. Sauté onions and mushrooms in butter until golden. Add seafood, sour cream, wine and Worcestershire. In a separate bowl, combine soup, flour and curry powder. Add to seafood mixture. Add noodles and place in a large flat buttered casserole. Cover with cheese and sprinkle with oregano and paprika. Bake uncovered for 30 to 45 minutes.

Ginger Scallops

2 tablespoons	finely chopped green onions
10 tablespoons	butter
1 large	carrot, julienned
2 tablespoons	finely chopped fresh ginger*
1/2 cup	dry white wine
1/2 cup	whipping cream
	salt and freshly ground pepper to taste
1 1/4 pounds	scallops

Sauté green onions in 2 tablespoons butter. Add carrots and cook 30 seconds. Add ginger. Stir in the wine. When thoroughly heated, add the cream, salt and pepper and cook over high heat until the sauce is reduced by half. Add scallops. Cook 1 minute. Stir in remaining butter and serve.

Buzzy's
Vermouth Scallops

Serves 4

By itself or served over rice, this dish is elegant.

1 – 1½ pounds	scallops
½ cup	dry vermouth
¼ cup	butter
½ teaspoon	salt
⅛ teaspoon	ground pepper
¼ teaspoon	paprika
4 – 5 cloves	garlic, minced
1 tablespoon	minced parsley
3 tablespoons	lemon juice

Marinate scallops in vermouth for several hours in the refrigerator. Heat 2 tablespoons butter in a large skillet. Add salt, pepper, paprika and garlic. Add scallops and cook quickly over high heat, stirring occasionally until golden brown (5 to 10 minutes). Transfer to a heated platter. To pan juices, add parsley, lemon juice and remaining butter. Heat and pour over scallops.

Abalone with Red Sauce

Serves 8 – 10

A spicy dish that accompanies a Korean meal.

> 1 pound   canned abalone
>> *Garnish: Watercress or Chinese parsley**

Slice abalone very thin and arrange on a platter. Garnish with watercress or Chinese parsley.

Red Sauce for dipping

1 teaspoon	Ko Choo Jung*
2¹/2 tablespoons	soy sauce
1 tablespoon	rice vinegar*
1 tablespoon	water
1/2 teaspoon	crushed garlic
1 teaspoon	sugar
1 teaspoon	sesame oil*
1 teaspoon	minced chives

Combine ingredients. Pour into individual dishes for dipping.

Gardenia
+
Bougainvillea

Vegetables

Artichoke Soufflé

Artichokes
6 large	artichokes
1 teaspoon	salt
2 tablespoons	lemon juice

Remove stems from base of artichokes. Trim about 2 inches off tops. Place in boiling salted water to cover. Add lemon juice. Cook 20 to 40 minutes or until leaves can be removed with slight pressure. Do not overcook. Drain, cool and remove inner leaves and choke. Pat dry and wrap foil around each artichoke to prevent drying out while baking.

Soufflé Filling
1^1/$_2$ cups	milk
6 tablespoons	butter
9 tablespoons	flour
6	egg yolks
3/4 pound	artichoke hearts, cooked and chopped
1/4 teaspoon	cayenne
1/4 teaspoon	nutmeg
2 tablespoons	minced green onion
4 tablespoons	grated Gruyère cheese
1/2 teaspoon	salt
8	egg whites

Bring milk and butter to a boil. Add flour and stir vigorously until mixture leaves sides of pan. Remove from heat. Beat in egg yolks one at a time, beating well after each addition. Add artichoke hearts, cayenne, nutmeg, onion, cheese and salt. (Mix may be refrigerated at this point until ready to bake. If refrigerated, bring to room tempereature before using.) Preheat oven to 375 degrees.

continued...

Beat egg whites until stiff. Mix $1/3$ of the egg whites into soufflé mix, then gently fold in remaining egg whites. Place foil-wrapped artichoke shells on a baking sheet and heat for three minutes. Remove and fill each shell $4/5$ full with mixture. Place in lower third of oven. Bake 40 to 50 minutes until soufflés rise and brown on top. Remove foil and serve immediately. Note: Canned or frozen artichoke hearts may be used for soufflé filling.

Alii Artichoke Casserole

Serves 8

3 (10-ounce) packages	frozen chopped spinach
2 (14-ounce) cans	artichoke hearts, drained and cut in half
8 ounces	cream cheese
$1/2$ cup	butter
2 tablespoons	Worcestershire sauce
1 teaspoon	salt
$1/2$ teaspoon	garlic powder
$1/2$ teaspoon	pepper
$1/8$ teaspoon	cayenne
$1/8$ teaspoon	Tabasco
1 tablespoon	lemon juice
$1/2$ cup	Italian-seasoned bread crumbs

Preheat oven to 350 degrees. Cook spinach and drain well. Melt the butter and cream cheese. Add seasonings, lemon juice and spinach, mixing after each addition. In a greased 2-quart casserole place a layer of artichoke hearts, then a layer of spinach mixture and repeat. Top with bread crumbs. Bake for 30 minutes.

Artichoke Elégante
Serves 4

8	artichoke bottoms
3 tablespoons	butter
1/2 pound	fresh mushrooms, thinly sliced
3/4 cup	Béchamel sauce (see index)
1 teaspoon	salt
1/2 teaspoon	pepper
1/3 to 1/2 cup	grated Gruyère cheese
2 – 3 tablespoons	butter

Preheat oven to 400 degrees. In a skillet, sauté artichoke bottoms in butter. Transfer to shallow casserole. Add mushrooms to skillet and sauté for 3 minutes. Combine mushrooms with Béchamel sauce, salt and pepper. Fill artichoke bottoms with mushroom mixture. Sprinkle cheese over top. Dot with butter and bake for 5 to 10 minutes.

Choi Sum with Oyster Sauce
Serves 4

1 bunch	choi sum* (approximately 1 pound)
1 tablespoon	vegetable oil
1 large clove	garlic, minced
3 tablespoons	oyster sauce*

Wash choi sum and cut into 3-inch lengths. (Don't shake off water). In a medium size pot, sauté garlic in oil. Add choi sum, cover and steam on high heat for 1 to 2 minutes or until bright green and limp. Add oyster sauce and stir to coat. Cook 1 minute longer. Serve.

Kula Carrots and Zucchini

Serves 8

3 tablespoons	butter
3 cloves	garlic, minced
5 medium	carrots, peeled and thinly sliced
3 small	zucchini, thinly sliced
1/4 teaspoon	rosemary
	salt and pepper to taste
1 tablespoon	water
1 tablespoon	capers

Melt butter in a frying pan over medium heat. Lightly sauté garlic. Add carrots and cook 2 minutes. Stir in zucchini, rosemary, salt and pepper. Cook until zucchini is heated through, then add 1 tablespoon of water and cover pan. Cook over medium heat until carrots are tender, stirring occasionally. Don't overcook. Stir in capers and serve.

Gingered Carrots

Serves 4

8 medium	carrots, peeled and quartered
1/2 teaspoon	salt
1	cinnamon stick
1 1/2 tablespoons	butter, melted
1/2 teaspoon	ground ginger
2 tablespoons	brown sugar
1 teaspoon	chopped parsley

Place carrots in saucepan with salt and cinnamon stick. Add water to cover. Simmer, covered, for 20 minutes or until tender but still crisp. Combine butter with ginger, sugar and parsley. Toss lightly with drained carrots.

Marinated Carrots

Serves 12

5 cups	sliced carrots, cooked but crisp
1	Maui onion,* sliced in rings
1	green pepper, seeded and cut into strips
1 cup	sugar
3/4 cup	red wine vinegar with garlic
1 tablespoon	prepared mustard
2 teaspoons	salt
1 teaspoon	pepper
2 teaspoons	garlic salt
1 (10 3/4-ounce) can	tomato soup
1/2 cup	vegetable oil
1 tablespoon	Worcestershire sauce

Place carrots, onions and green pepper in a large bowl. In a separate bowl, mix remaining ingredients and pour over vegetables. Cover and marinate in refrigerator 12 hours. Note: Marinated vegetables will keep in refrigerator for 2 to 3 weeks. Marinade can also be used as salad dressing.

Potato Pie
Serves 4—6

The humble potato dressed up for company.

1 cup	Half and Half
24 ounces	frozen hash browns, thawed for 20 minutes
1/2 cup	butter
1/2 cup	minced onion
1 teaspoon	salt
1/2 teaspoon	pepper
1/4 cup	grated Parmesan cheese

Preheat oven to 350 degrees. Bring cream to a boil and add potatoes. Cook until cream is absorbed. Mix in remaining ingredients, except cheese. Put mixture into a greased pie plate. Cover with cheese. Bake uncovered for 1 hour.

Roësti Potatoes
Serves 2

1/4 cup	butter
1 teaspoon	chopped onion
1/2 slice	bacon, chopped
1 cup	grated cooked potatoes

Sauté onion and bacon in butter until bacon is crisp and onion is transparent. Add potatoes, forming a large patty in skillet. Brown evenly on both sides until crisp and golden.

Martin Wyss
Swiss Inn
Honolulu, Hawaii

Ono
Sweet Potatoes

Serves 4 – 6

An old favorite with a tropical taste.

1 (24-ounce) can	sweet potatoes or yams, drained
3	ripe bananas
1 teaspoon	cinnamon
1/2 teaspoon	salt
	brown sugar
1/4 cup	macadamia nut bits*
1/4 cup	crushed corn flakes
1/4 cup	melted butter

Preheat oven to 350 degrees. Mash sweet potatoes and bananas with cinnamon and salt. Place in a baking dish. Top with a thin layer of brown sugar. Mix nuts and corn flakes. Spread over brown sugar. Pour melted butter over top. Bake for 45 to 50 minutes.

Snow Peas
Kahala Style

Serves 4–6

2 tablespoons	peanut oil
12 – 14	water chestnuts,* sliced 1/4 inch thick
1 cup	thinly sliced fresh mushrooms
1 cup	diced onion
3/4 pound	fresh snow peas*
or	
3 (6-ounce) packages	frozen Chinese peas*
1 teaspoon	salt
1 tablespoon	soy sauce
1 tablespoon	water
1/2 teaspoon	garlic salt

In a wok* or large skillet with a tight fitting cover, sauté water chestnuts, mushrooms and onion in peanut oil for 5 minutes or until onion is tender. Add snow peas, salt, soy sauce and water. Mix well. Sprinkle with garlic salt. Cover tightly and simmer 5 minutes or until snow peas are tender but still crisp.

Broccoli Ring

2 pounds	fresh broccoli, chopped
or	
4 (10-ounce) packages	frozen chopped broccoli
1/4 cup	butter
1/4 cup	finely chopped onion
3 tablespoons	flour
1 teaspoon	seasoned salt
1 cup	whipping cream
1 teaspoon	instant chicken bouillon
3	eggs, well beaten
1/2 cup	mayonnaise
1/4 cup	chopped parsley

Preheat oven to 350 degrees. Cook broccoli in boiling water until tender. Drain. Sauté onion in butter until golden. Blend in flour, salt, cream and bouillon, stirring until sauce comes to a boil and thickens. Blend a small amount of the sauce into the eggs. Add egg mixture to sauce and cook for two minutes. Remove from heat. Fold in mayonnaise, parsley and drained broccoli. Spoon into a well greased 5-cup ring mold. Set mold in pan of hot water and bake for 35 to 40 minutes or until knife inserted in center comes out clean. Let stand 1 to 2 minutes before unmolding. Center may be filled with creamed mushrooms or tomatoes.

Candied Tomatoes

Makes 1 1/2 — 2 quarts

This is a delicious accompaniment to prime rib, pork roast or lamb.

3 (28-ounce) cans	whole tomatoes
2 small	onions, finely chopped
3/4 – 1 cup	sugar
1/2 cup	butter
1 teaspoon	garlic salt

Place all ingredients in a deep 4-quart saucepan and boil for 30 minutes. Lower heat until mixture barely bubbles. Simmer for 7 to 8 hours. Preheat oven to 325 degrees and bake in buttered casserole for 15 to 20 minutes. Variation: Place a portion of mixture in large buttered mushroom caps and bake in a preheated 325 degree oven for 5 to 7 minutes.

Ultimate Zucchini

Serves 8

A marinated cold vegetable that is excellent with egg or pasta main dishes.

1 cup	chili sauce
2 teaspoons	grated Parmesan cheese
3 tablespoons	red wine vinegar
2 tablespoons	olive oil
1/4 teaspoon	garlic powder
1/4 teaspoon	oregano
1/4 teaspoon	pepper
1/4 – 1/2 teaspoon	salt
	juice of 1/2 lemon
4 large	zucchini

Combine ingredients, except zucchini, to make marinade. Set aside. Slice zucchini 1/8-inch thick. Place in glass bowl and pour marinade over zucchini. Chill 4 hours, turning several times.

219

Curried Onion Casserole

Serve with turkey or ham.

2 pounds	small white boiling onions
1/3 cup	butter
1/4 cup	flour
dash	cayenne
1/2 teaspoon	curry powder
1/2 teaspoon	paprika
1/4 teaspoon	pepper
1 cup	beef bouillon
1 cup	milk
1/2 cup	grated sharp Cheddar cheese

Preheat oven to 350 degrees. Peel onions and cook in boiling salted water for 15 minutes. Drain and place in a buttered casserole. Melt butter in a saucepan. Add flour and seasonings and blend. Add bouillon and milk, stirring constantly until mixture is thick and smooth. Add cheese and stir until melted. Pour over onions. Bake for 30 minutes.

Hidden Palm

3 pounds	frozen French style green beans
1 – 1^1/$_2$ teaspoons	garlic salt
^{1}/$_4$ – ^{1}/$_2$ teaspoon	pepper
3 tablespoons	butter
^{3}/$_4$ cup	diced celery
1 (14-ounce) can	hearts of palm
^{3}/$_4$ cup	mayonnaise
1 (6-ounce) can	pitted small ripe olives (optional)

Garnish: Paprika

Preheat oven to 350 degrees. Cook green beans until warm but still crunchy. Season with garlic salt, pepper and 1^1/$_2$ tablespoons butter. Sauté celery in remaining butter until tender. Cut hearts of palm into bite-size pieces. Combine beans, celery, hearts of palm and mayonnaise. Add olives. Bake in a 2^1/$_2$—3-quart greased casserole for 20 to 30 minutes. Sprinkle with paprika before serving. Note: This can be made a day in advance and heated before serving.

Italian Marinated Vegetables

Serves 8

1(8-ounce) can	button mushrooms
1	green pepper, cut into ½-inch strips
1	carrot, chopped
2 cups	cauliflower flowerets
1 (14-ounce) can	artichoke hearts, drained
12	green onions, chopped
½ cup	pimiento stuffed olives
1½ cups	red wine vinegar
1 teaspoon	sugar
1½ teaspoons	salt
½ teaspoon	pepper
2 teaspoons	oregano
2 teaspoons	crushed red pepper flakes
2 tablespoons	Dijon mustard
½ cup	olive oil
12 ounces	cherry tomatoes, cut in half
2 tablespoons	minced parsley

Combine mushrooms, green pepper, carrot, cauliflower, artichokes, onions and olives. Heat vinegar and stir in sugar and seasonings. Cool slightly, then add oil. Pour over vegetables and mix. Cover and refrigerate for 24 hours, stirring periodically. Add tomatoes and parsley when ready to serve.

Eurasian Vegetables   *Serves 4 — 6*

2 tablespoons	vegetable oil
2 – 3 cloves	garlic, crushed
1/2 pound	green beans cut in 2-inch pieces
1/2 cup	sliced water chestnuts*
1 teaspoon	tarragon
1 teaspoon	basil
	freshly ground pepper
1 teaspoon	salt
2 tablespoons	wine
1	red sweet bell pepper, seeded and sliced
2 – 3	green onions, finely sliced on the diagonal
3 – 4	sliced mushrooms (optional)
1 tablespoon	white vinegar
1 teaspoon	chopped parsley
	Garnish: Parsley sprigs

Heat vegetable oil in a wok* or skillet. Add garlic and stir-fry for 1 minute. Discard garlic. Stir-fry beans 2 to 3 minutes. Add water chestnuts, tarragon, basil, pepper, salt and wine. Then add red pepper, onions, mushrooms, vinegar and parsley. Stir-fry briefly. Place in serving dish and decorate with additional sprigs of parsley.

Nino J. Martin
The International Chef⊙
Hawaii Public Television
Honolulu, Hawaii

223

Cauliflower and Watercress Purée

A dish honoring Oahu's Sumida Watercress Farm near Pearl Harbor, home of cress so succulent that a large regional shopping center was split and connected by monorail in order to preserve the farm.

1 head	cauliflower, separated into flowerets
1 bunch	watercress, trimmed
4 tablespoons	butter
5 tablespoons	flour
2 cups	Half and Half, heated to a boil
1/2 cup	grated Gruyère cheese
1/2 cup	whipping cream
1 teaspoon	salt
1/2 teaspoon	pepper
dash	nutmeg
2 tablespoons	grated Gruyère cheese
1/4 cup	fine breadcrumbs
2 tablespoons	butter, melted

Preheat oven to 375 degrees. Place cauliflower and watercress in a saucepan filled with 2 cups of rapidly boiling water. Boil for 5 minutes or until tender. Drain. Purée cauliflower and watercress in a food mill (not a food processor) to maintain the texture. In a saucepan, melt butter and slowly stir in flour. Add Half and Half, stirring mixture until smooth and thick. Fold in 1/2 cup Gruyère cheese. Add cream, salt, pepper and nutmeg. Add the purée. Place in baking dish. Combine bread crumbs with remaining cheese and butter. Sprinkle evenly on top of purée and bake for 25 minutes. Serve hot. Note: Can be made 1 or 2 days ahead and refrigerated until ready to bake.

Zucchini Cups   *Serves 8*

1 tablespoon	butter
1 tablespoon	olive oil
1/2 cup	chopped mushrooms
4	green onions, chopped
2 large cloves	garlic, minced
1 cup	ground ham
or	
1 (6-ounce) can	deviled ham
1 (14-ounce) can	artichoke hearts, finely chopped
1 1/2 cups	bread crumbs
1/2 cup	minced parsley
1 teaspoon	basil
1/2 teaspoon	rosemary
1 teaspoon	anchovy paste
2 teaspoons	lemon juice
1/2 cup	grated Romano cheese
1/2 teaspoon	freshly ground pepper
	salt to taste
3 pounds	zucchini
1/4 cup	olive oil

Heat butter and 1 tablespoon of oil. Quickly sauté the mushrooms and green onions. In a large bowl, combine all remaining ingredients except zucchini and olive oil. Stir in sautéed mixture and mix thoroughly. Preheat oven to 350 degrees. Wash the zucchini and cut into 3-inch lengths. Scoop out the centers, leaving a shell about 1/4-inch thick. Stuff zucchini with mixture and arrange in a large shallow baking pan. Drizzle with oil. Cover and bake for 30 minutes or until zucchini is tender.

Cleo Evans
Cooking Instructor
Honolulu, Hawaii

225

Zucchini Custard
Serves 8

2 pounds	zucchini, sliced but not peeled
2²/3 cups	grated Cheddar cheese
4	eggs, slightly beaten
1 cup	milk
1/2 teaspoon	salt
1/4 teaspoon	pepper
1/3 teaspoon	dry mustard
1/2 clove	garlic, minced

Preheat oven to 325 degrees. Parboil zucchini. Drain. Line a buttered casserole dish with half of the cheese. Cover with zucchini slices. Combine eggs, milk, salt, pepper, mustard and garlic. Pour over zucchini. Cover with remaining cheese. Bake for 45 minutes or until custard is set.

Asparagus Sesame
Serves 6

2 pounds	fresh asparagus
2 tablespoons	vegetable oil
1 tablespoon	sesame oil*
1 tablespoon	soy sauce
2 teaspoons	brown sugar

Garnish: Toasted sesame seeds

Trim ends from asparagus. Place spears in a bowl for steaming. Mix oils, soy sauce and sugar. Pour over asparagus. Steam* covered for 15 minutes. Garnish. Note: Asparagus may be served in spears or cut in 2-inch diagonal pieces.

upright
Heliconia

Eggs, Cheese, Rice and Pasta

Artichoke Quiche

Serves 6

1 (9-inch)	pie shell
2 tablespoons	butter
1/2 cup	chopped green onion
2	eggs
1 tablespoon	flour
2/3 cup	Half and Half
1/4 teaspoon	garlic salt
1 (14-ounce) can	artichoke hearts, drained and coarsely chopped
1 cup	grated Hot Pepper cheese
1 cup	grated Cheddar cheese

Preheat oven to 400 degrees. Pierce bottom of pie shell and bake for 12 minutes. Reduce oven to 350 degrees. In a small skillet sauté the onion in butter. In a large bowl, beat the eggs, flour and cream together. Stir in the garlic salt, artichokes, Hot Pepper cheese, Cheddar cheese and the onion-butter mixture. Stir until well blended. Pour into the pastry shell and bake for 45 minutes or until firm in the center.

Aussie Quiche   *Serves 6*

Pastry

2 cups	self rising flour
1/2 cup	melted butter
1	egg, beaten

Mix together with a fork. Press into a 9-inch pie plate. Chill while preparing filling.

Filling

1 pound	mushrooms, thickly sliced
1 bunch	green onions, chopped
2 tablespoons	butter
	salt and pepper to taste
1 tablespoon	lemon juice

Sauté mushrooms and onions in butter for 2 to 3 minutes. Season. Cool slightly and stir in lemon juice. Preheat oven to 350 degrees.

Topping

1 cup	cottage cheese
1	egg
1 1/2 cups	grated Cheddar cheese

Combine topping ingredients. Put mushroom filling into pastry and top with cheese mixture. Bake for 40 minutes until light brown. Let stand 10 minutes before serving.

Hamburger Quiche

1 (9-inch)	unbaked pie shell
1 pound	lean ground beef
2 cups	grated sharp Cheddar cheese
1/2 cup	mayonnaise
1/2 cup	milk
2	eggs
1 tablespoon	cornstarch
1 cup	sliced green onions
1 pound	mushrooms, sliced
	salt and pepper

Preheat oven to 350 degrees. Brown meat and drain. Combine cheese, mayonnaise, milk, eggs and cornstarch. Stir in onions, mushrooms and beef. Add salt and pepper. Pour into pie shell and bake 40 to 45 minutes until puffy and golden brown.

Wine and Shallot Quiche   *Serves 6*

1 (9-inch)	deep dish pie shell
8 ounces	grated Gruyère cheese
1/2 cup	white wine
1/4 cup	minced shallots
4	eggs
2 cups	whipping cream
3/4 teaspoon	salt
1/8 teaspoon	white pepper
dash	nutmeg
dash	cayenne

Preheat oven to 400 degrees. Bake pie shell for 5 minutes. Sprinkle grated cheese evenly over pie shell. In a saucepan, bring white wine and shallots to a boil. Lower heat and simmer for 3 minutes. Cool. Mix remaining ingredients in a blender. Add wine and shallots and pour entire mixture over cheese in pie shell. Bake for 25 to 30 minutes or until golden brown.

Albert Schmid
Executive Chef
Dillingham Corporation
Honolulu, Hawaii

233

Seafood Quiche

Makes 2 quiches

2 (9-inch)	deep dish pie shells
6 ounces	frozen king crabmeat, thawed and drained
1¹/₂ cups	shrimp, cooked, shelled, deveined and chopped
1 pound	Swiss cheese, grated
¹/₂ – 1 cup	finely chopped celery
¹/₂ cup	finely chopped green onion
1 cup	mayonnaise
2 tablespoons	flour
¹/₂ – 1 cup	dry white wine
4	eggs, slightly beaten

Preheat oven to 350 degrees. Combine crabmeat, shrimp, cheese, celery, and green onion. Divide seafood mixture equally between pie shells. Combine mayonnaise, flour, white wine and eggs. Divide mayonnaise mixture equally between pie shells, pouring evenly over seafood. Bake 40 to 45 minutes or until firm in center. Note: If quiches are to be frozen, do not bake before freezing.

Spinach Pie

This is a delight to the eye and the palate.

1 (9-inch)	deep dish pie shell, baked
1 (10-ounce) package	frozen spinach
3 tablespoons	butter
1 small	onion, minced
1 – 2 cloves	garlic, minced
2 cups	finely chopped mushrooms
4	eggs
8 ounces	cream cheese, softened
8 ounces	Kasseri cheese, grated
8 ounces	feta cheese, crumbled
1 cup	grated Swiss cheese
1/4 – 1/3 cup	grated Parmesan cheese

Preheat oven to 350 degrees. Thaw and drain spinach. Sauté onion and garlic in butter. Add mushrooms and cook for 3 to 5 minutes. Drain juices and set aside. Combine eggs and cream cheese. In bottom of pie shell, layer 1/3 of the Kasseri, all of the garlic, onion and mushroom mixture, 1/2 of the egg and cream cheese mix, balance of Kasseri, all of the spinach (squeezing out all excess water), crumbled feta cheese, balance of egg mixture, all of the Swiss cheese and all of the Parmesan cheese. Bake for 45 minutes.

Spinach Soufflé Roll

Serves 8 as an entrée, 12 as a pupu*

Soufflé Roll

4 tablespoons	butter
1/2 cup	flour
1/8 teaspoon	salt
2 cups	milk, heated
5	egg yolks, beaten
2 teaspoons	sugar
1/8 teaspoon	nutmeg
4	egg whites, stiffly beaten, but not dry

Preheat oven to 325 degrees. Melt butter, add flour and salt and stir until smooth. Add milk gradually and cook for 5 minutes, stirring constantly. Add a small amount to egg yolks, stir, then add yolks to heated mixture. Remove from heat. Add sugar and nutmeg. Fold in egg whites. Grease a 10 x 15-inch jelly roll pan, line with waxed paper and grease again. Flour generously. Spread batter evenly over pan and bake for 25 to 30 minutes or until golden brown. Remove from oven and let stand 10 minutes. Turn out on a clean towel covered with overlapping pieces of waxed paper cut slightly larger than pan. Peel paper carefully from roll.

Filling

2 tablespoons	butter
4	green onions, chopped
4 medium	mushrooms, sliced
1 cup	chopped spinach, cooked and drained until dry
1 cup	chopped ham
1 tablespoon	Dijon mustard
1/4 teaspoon	nutmeg
6 ounces	cream cheese
	salt and pepper to taste
	Garnish: Parsley sprigs

continued...

Sauté green onions and mushrooms in butter. Add spinach, ham, mustard, nutmeg, cream cheese, salt and pepper. Stir until well mixed. Heat until warm. Gently spread over soufflé roll. Roll from small end, placing seam side down. Slice and serve.

Krasnapolski
Serves 6—8

A light easy spinach soufflé.

6	eggs
2 (10-ounce) packages	chopped spinach, thawed and drained
1/2 cup	melted butter
1 (32-ounce) carton	cottage cheese
1 pound	sharp Cheddar cheese, grated
2 tablespoons	flour

Preheat oven to 350 degrees. Beat eggs. Add spinach, butter, cottage cheese and Cheddar cheese. Sprinkle flour over ingredients and blend. Bake for 1 hour in a greased 3-quart casserole.

Roquefort Soufflé

3½ tablespoons	butter
3 tablespoons	flour
1 cup	milk
	salt and white pepper
1 cup	crumbled Roquefort cheese
3 cups	egg whites

Preheat oven to 375 degrees. Melt butter in saucepan. Remove from heat and lightly brush soufflé dishes. Add flour to remaining butter and mix well. Bring milk to a boil and add to the butter-flour mixture. Season and chill. Add Roquefort cheese 20 minutes before final preparation. Beat egg whites until firm. Mix one heaping tablespoon of egg whites into batter. Fold in the remaining egg whites. Fill dishes half full and bake for 12 minutes. Serve immediately.

Bagwell's
Hyatt Regency Hotel
Honolulu, Hawaii

Chili Cheese Fritatta
Serves 6

2 (7-ounce) cans	green chilies, seeded
1 pound	Swiss cheese, grated
1 pound	Cheddar cheese, grated
3 tablespoons	Wondra
3/4 cup	evaporated milk
4	eggs, beaten
1 (7-ounce) can	green chili salsa

Preheat oven to 350 degrees. Butter an 11-inch quiche pan. Set aside. Combine the two cheeses. Alternately layer the chilies and cheese in the pan. In a blender, mix flour, milk and eggs. Pour this mixture over the chilies and cheese. Bake for 30 minutes. Remove from oven and top with salsa. Bake an additional 15 to 20 minutes. Cool about 10 minutes to allow the cheese to set.

Cottage Cheese Soufflé
Serves 4

3	eggs, lightly beaten
2 cups	cottage cheese
1/2 pound	grated Cheddar cheese
2 tablespoons	melted butter
	salt and pepper to taste
1/4 cup	minced onion
2	thin slices of onion, separated into rings

Preheat oven to 325 degrees. Combine eggs, cottage cheese, Cheddar cheese, butter and seasonings. Stir until ingredients are blended and pour into a 9 x 9-inch baking dish. Top with onion rings. Cook for one hour or until top is slightly browned and inside is set. Note: Stir, do not use electric mixer.

Fried Rice
Serves 6

A great way to use leftover rice.

2 tablespoons	butter
1/2 cup	finely chopped onion
1 clove	garlic, minced
1/4 cup	finely chopped carrot
1/2 cup	finely chopped water chestnuts*
4 cups	cooked rice
1/3 cup	soy sauce
1 teaspoon	sugar
1 teaspoon	sake*
1 teaspoon	chopped fresh ginger*
or	
1/2 teaspoon	ground ginger
1 cup	chopped green onions
1/2 cup	minced ham or bacon
2	egg omelet, julienned

Sauté the onion, garlic, carrot and water chestnuts in butter. Add the rice and fry for 3 minutes. In a small bowl, combine soy sauce, sugar, sake and ginger. Stir sauce into rice. When ready to serve, stir in green onions, ham or bacon and eggs. Note: Variations are endless. Use leftover vegetables and meats and create your own family favorites.

Barley Pilaf

1/2 cup	butter
1 3/4 cups	pearl barley
2 medium	onions, finely chopped
8 ounces	fresh mushrooms, sliced
4 cups	chicken or beef broth
1/2 cup	toasted macadamia nut bits*
1/2 cup	chopped parsley

Preheat oven to 350 degrees. Sauté barley until golden in 4 tablespoons butter. Spoon into a large buttered casserole. Sauté onions and mushrooms in remaining butter and stir into barley. Pour two cups of broth over barley mixture, cover tightly and bake for 45 minutes. Add remaining liquid and bake uncovered 45 minutes longer, stirring occasionally. Fifteen minutes before serving, stir in macadamia nuts and parsley. Note: If mixture becomes dry, add more liquid.

241

Sizzling Rice
Serves 4

This dish sings and sizzles and is very dramatic.

1 cup	long grain rice
4 cups	water
2 teaspoons	salt
	vegetable oil

Cook rice in water until done. Spread rice evenly on a well-greased rimmed cookie sheet. Bake in a 250 degree oven for approximately 8 hours, occasionally turning rice with a spatula. Break into bite-size pieces. Just before serving, heat oil in a pan and fry until golden brown, approximately 4 minutes. Remove with a slotted spoon and drain on a paper towel. Transfer to a heated dish. Bring to the table and immediately spoon into hot chicken broth or other soup. If sizzling rice is being served with a shrimp or scallop entree, place rice on a heated platter and spoon entrée over rice.

Ono Rice
Serves 4

A seasoned rice that is tasty with chicken dishes.

$2^1/_2$ tablespoons	butter
$1^1/_2$ tablespoons	finely chopped onion
1 cup	long grain rice, uncooked
$1/_8$ teaspoon	Tabasco
$1^1/_2$ cups	chicken broth
$1/_2$	bay leaf
2 sprigs	parsley, chopped

Preheat oven to 425 degrees. Melt the butter in an oven-proof casserole. Add onion and sauté until clear. Add rice and cook for 30 seconds. Add the remaining ingredients and bring to a boil. Cover the casserole. Place in the oven and bake for 20 to 30 minutes.

Sunset Rice
Serves 6

1 cup	mochi rice*
1 cup	rice
1/2 pound	Lup Cheong,* steamed and cut in bite-size pieces
1/2 pound	char siu,* cut in bite-size pieces
1 (5-ounce) can	mushrooms, including liquid
2 cups	chicken broth
	Garnish: Chopped green onion

Preheat oven to 350 degrees. Combine rice in a 3-quart casserole. Add remaining ingredients. Cover and bake for 1 hour. Garnish.

Double Creamed Noodles
Serves 6—8

1 pound medium-size	noodles, cooked al dente and drained
8 ounces	cream cheese, softened
2 cups	Half and Half
1/2 cup	grated Gruyère cheese
3/4 teaspoon	salt
1/2 teaspoon	garlic salt
1/3 teaspoon	white pepper
1/2 cup	chopped fresh parsley
	butter

Preheat oven to 350 degrees. Combine ingredients. Place in a 2 1/2-quart casserole and dot with butter. Bake uncovered for 20 minutes or until the top is golden brown.

Furikake Pan Sushi

Serves 10—12

A simple Oriental rice treat that is full of flavor as well as color.

1/2 cup	rice vinegar*
1/2 cup	sugar
1 teaspoon	salt
8 cups	hot cooked white rice

Combine vinegar, sugar and salt, stirring until sugar is dissolved. Pour over rice and mix until well absorbed. Press into a 9 x 13-inch pan. Precut into 3 x 3-inch servings.

Topping

3	egg omelet, julienned
1 (.85-ounce) bottle	furikake*
1/4 cup	pickled ginger slivers*
1/2 cup	fish cake strips*
6 – 8	stringbeans, blanched and julienned
1/2 cup	julienned ham, chicken or turkey
2 tablespoons	green hana ebi*
2 tablespoons	red hana ebi*

Sprinkle ingredients evenly over rice. Cover pan with foil until ready to serve. Do not refrigerate as rice will dry out.

Chow Fun
Serves 4 — 6

1 tablespoon	vegetable oil
½ pound	char siu,* sliced in thin strips
1 tablespoon	finely chopped fresh ginger*
2 teaspoons	salt (optional)
2 tablespoons	oyster sauce*
2 tablespoons	soy sauce
2 cups	bean sprouts*
1 stalk	celery, thinly sliced
1-2	carrots, julienned
2	green onions, finely sliced
7 ounces	Chow Fun noodles,* cooked and drained
¼ pound	ham, julienned
2	egg omelet, julienned
	*Garnish: 2 tablespoons sesame seeds, Chinese parsley**

Heat oil in skillet until almost smoking. Fry char siu for 1 minute. Add ginger, salt, oyster sauce and soy sauce and sauté 1 minute. Add vegetables and stir-fry for 2 minutes. Add noodles and heat for 2 minutes, stirring occasionally. Put mixture on a platter. Add ham and eggs. Toss lightly. Garnish.

Parmesan-Zucchini Pasta *Serves 4*

1 (8-ounce) package thin egg noodles, cooked
3 tablespoons vegetable oil
1 pound zucchini, julienned
2 tablespoons butter
1 tablespoon flour
1 cup milk
3 ounces fresh Parmesan cheese, grated
1 teaspoon dry basil
1/4 teaspoon salt

Heat 1 tablespoon of oil in a skillet. Add zucchini and cook until soft. Remove zucchini from skillet. Add remaining oil and butter. Stir in flour and cook for 1 minute. Gradually add milk, stirring constantly. Add zucchini, cheese, basil and salt. Toss until cheese is melted and sauce is smooth. Serve immediately over noodles.

Helen's Pasta *Serves 6*

Great with broiled lamb chops.

1 (28-ounce) can Italian plum tomatoes
or
3 whole tomatoes, cubed
1 1/2 teaspoons salt
1 teaspoon pepper
2 cloves fresh garlic, minced
1 cup fresh basil, loosely packed
1/4 cup olive oil
1 (10-ounce) package large pasta shells, cooked

Break up tomatoes, add salt, pepper, garlic, basil and olive oil. Marinate for 1 hour or longer. Cook shells al dente. Rinse. Pour sauce over hot pasta.

Crab Mushroom
Spaghetti Sauce

Serves 6

6 ounces	crab
1 cup	chopped onions
1 clove	garlic, minced
1/2 pound	fresh mushrooms, sliced
1/4 cup	butter
2 tablespoons	flour
1 teaspoon	salt
dash	pepper
1/2 teaspoon	oregano
2 cups	Half and Half
1 pound	vermicelli, cooked

Garnish: 3 tablespoons chopped parsley and grated Parmesan cheese

Drain and slice crab. Sauté onions, garlic and mushrooms in butter until tender. Blend in flour and seasonings. Stir in cream and cook until slightly thickened, stirring constantly. Add crab and cook until heated thoroughly. Serve over vermicelli. Garnish.

Fettucini and Peaches   *Serves 6*

8 ounces	fettucini, white or green
1 teaspoon	salt
1 teaspoon	vegetable oil
1/2 cup	whipping cream
1	egg yolk
1 cup	grated Romano cheese
1 tablespoon	minced parsley
1 cup	sliced firm fresh peaches
1/2 cup	julienned ham or sliced prosciutto ham

Garnish: Nutmeg

Boil fettucini in salted water and vegetable oil for approximately 12 minutes or until tender. Drain well. In a saucepan, lightly beat cream, egg yolk and cheese. Heat the mixture until hot. Combine fettucini, parsley, peaches, ham and hot cheese mixture and toss lightly. Garnish and serve immediately.

Ginger

Sauces, Condiments and Da Kine

Makaiwa
Mango Sauce

Makes 1 gallon

Makaiwa Street in Kahala is well-known for the variety of fruits and flowering trees growing there.

3 quarts	ripe mangoes,* peeled and sliced
2-inch piece	fresh ginger,* peeled
1 cup	sliced green pepper
4 cloves	garlic, minced
1/4 teaspoon	cayenne
1 pound	onions, sliced
3 cups	vinegar
2 teaspoons	Angostura bitters
1 teaspoon	Tabasco
4 teaspoons	ground allspice
3 teaspoons	cumin
2 teaspoons	ground cloves
1 tablespoon	salt
6 cups	sugar

Blend mangoes, ginger and green pepper in food processor or blender until smooth. Combine sauce and remaining ingredients in a large, heavy pot. Simmer uncovered for 3 hours, stirring occasionally until thick. Pour into sterilized jars and seal immediately. Note: Refrigerate after opening. Serve with meats and poultry.

Sauce Albert

Makes 2 cups

A spicy mayonnaise sauce.

2 cups	mayonnaise
1 teaspoon	paprika
1 teaspoon	dry English mustard
2 tablespoons	lemon juice
	cayenne to taste

Combine ingredients and refrigerate. Serve chilled with Chicken Aspic (see index).

Albert Schmid
Executive Chef
Dillingham Corp
Honolulu, Hawaii

Sophie's Choice

Makes 1¹/2 cups

A sauce for ham, beef or poultry.

¹/2 cup	mayonnaise
2 tablespoons	prepared horseradish
2 tablespoons	guava* jelly, softened
1 teaspoon	dry English mustard
1 tablespoon	tarragon vinegar
¹/4 teaspoon	salt
2 drops	Tabasco
¹/2 cup	whipping cream, whipped
1 tablespoon	dry sherry

Combine mayonnaise and horseradish. Add guava jelly, dry mustard, vinegar, salt and Tabasco and blend well. Fold in whipped cream. Add sherry just before serving.

253

Cranberry Mandarin Sauce

Makes 3¹/₂ — 4 quarts

A colorful and tasty addition to your turkey dinner.

1 cup	honey
3 cups	brown sugar or raw sugar
4 cups	water
8 cups	fresh cranberries
4	tangerines or oranges
	Garnish: Mint or parsley

Boil honey, sugar and water for 5 minutes. Add cranberries and boil without stirring until skins pop, about 5 minutes. Remove from heat. Peel, section and seed tangerines, add to sauce and cool. To serve, use v-shaped melon cutter and cut through to centers of lemons or oranges, resulting in a "rick rack" edge. Hollow out shells and fill with cranberry mandarin sauce. Garnish tops with mint or parsley. Note: This recipe can easily be divided in half to make 2 quarts.

Compleat Kitchen
Honolulu, Hawaii

Soy and Hot Mustard Dipping Sauce

Makes 1/3 cup

1 teaspoon	dry hot mustard
1/2 teaspoon	water
1/3 cup	soy sauce

Mix dry mustard with water to form a paste. Let stand 15 minutes. Stir in soy sauce. Serve with Sashimi and Crispy Won Ton (see index).

Hawaiian Barbecue Sauce

Makes 6 cups

Use for basting or marinating poultry, pork or beef.

2 cups	olive oil
1 cup	catsup
1 cup	soy sauce
1/2 cup	brown sugar
2 tablespoons	salt
1 cup	chopped celery
1 cup	chopped onion
3 cloves	garlic, crushed
1 teaspoon	minced fresh ginger*
1 tablespoon	chili sauce

Mix all ingredients in a saucepan. Bring to a boil, stirring occasionally. Reduce heat and simmer for one hour.

Sweet and Sour Sauce

Makes 2 cups

Great for barbecues or as a dip for won ton. *

5 tablespoons	sugar
1 tablespoon	cornstarch
3 tablespoons	vinegar
2 tablespoons	Worcestershire sauce
4 tablespoons	catsup
1 1/2 cups	water

Combine ingredients in a saucepan and cook over moderate heat until thick. Serve warm as a dipping sauce or use to baste meat before grilling.

Sweet Sour Lumpia Sauce

Makes 2 cups

1 cup	water
1/2 cup	sugar
1/4 cup	vinegar
1/2 cup	catsup
2 teaspoons	soy sauce
dash	Tabasco
	salt and pepper to taste
2 tablespoons	cornstarch
1/4 cup	water

In a saucepan, bring water, sugar and vinegar to a boil. Add catsup, soy sauce, Tabasco, salt and pepper. Dissolve cornstarch in water and add to sauce. Cook until thickened. Serve with Lumpia (see index).

Char Siu Sauce

Makes 1 cup

A tasty marinade for pork, spareribs or chicken.

1 cup	brown sugar
1/4 cup	soy sauce
1/2 teaspoon	sesame oil*
1/8 teaspoon	Chinese Five Spice*
1 clove	garlic, minced
2 teaspoons	sherry
1 tablespoon	hoisin sauce*
1 tablespoon	red food coloring

Combine ingredients and mix well. Marinate meat overnight. Note: Meat should bake in a foil lined broiler pan at 350 degrees. Bake ribs for 30 minutes, pork and chicken for one hour.

Teriyaki Sauce Marinade

Makes 2 cups

Great for grilling, broiling or barbecue.

1 cup	soy sauce
1/2 cup	water
1/4 cup	mirin*
1/3 cup	brown sugar
1/2 cup	sugar
1 tablespoon	minced garlic
1 tablespoon	minced fresh ginger*

Combine ingredients in a saucepan and heat until the sugars dissolve. Cool marinade before using. This recipe makes enough to marinate 3 to 4 pounds of meat, ribs or chicken.

257

Fish Marinade

Makes 1 cup

Especially good on red meat fish.

1/3 cup	olive oil
1/3 cup	soy sauce
2 tablespoons	steak sauce
2 teaspoons	Worcestershire sauce
2 cloves	garlic, minced

Combine ingredients in a flat pan and marinate fish fillets for 45 minutes. If marinated longer, fish will taste very salty. Barbecue or broil the fish.

Remoulade Sauce

Makes 2 cups

Serve over seafood.

2 tablespoons	lemon juice
4 tablespoons	tarragon vinegar
3 cloves	garlic, minced
2 tablespoons	prepared mustard
2 tablespoons	creole mustard*
4 tablespoons	horseradish
2 teaspoons	salt
1 teaspoon	pepper
2 teaspoons	paprika
	cayenne to taste
1 cup	olive oil
1/2 cup	chopped celery
1/2 cup	chopped green onion

Combine lemon juice, vinegar and seasonings. Gradually add olive oil and stir with fork or rotary beater to blend well. Add celery and onions. Chill.

Blender Hollandaise

Makes 2/3 cup

3 large	egg yolks
1 tablespoon	fresh lemon juice
1/8 teaspoon	cayenne
1/2 cup	hot melted butter

Combine egg yolks, lemon juice and cayenne in blender. Mix lightly, just to break yolks. Turn blender on high and gradually add butter in a steady stream. Blend on high for 60 seconds and turn off for 30 seconds. Repeat this process until sauce thickens to a consistency where it does not drip from the spoon. Note: It is important that the butter be hot in order to cook yolks. On-off cycle may have to be repeated as many as 10 to 12 times.

Béchamel Sauce

Serves 4

1 1/2 tablespoons	butter
2 1/2 tablespoons	flour
1 cup	milk, heated to boiling

Melt butter in a saucepan. Add flour and mix well. Cook mixture for 3 minutes. Add milk, stirring constantly, until mixture thickens, about 3 minutes.

Newburg Sauce

Makes 3 cups

2 tablespoons butter
2 tablespoons flour
3/4 teaspoon salt
dash cayenne
2 cups Half and Half
4 egg yolks, well beaten
1/4 cup sherry

Melt butter, stir in flour, salt and cayenne. When well blended, add Half and Half and cook over low heat until sauce is smooth, just to boiling. Stir a little of the sauce into the egg yolks, mixing well. Blend in the rest of the sauce and add sherry.

Salsa Cocina

Makes 1 cup

This is a zippy dip for corn or tortilla chips.

3 large tomatoes
1/4 – 1/2 Maui onion*
6 – 7 green onions
3 fresh or canned hot green chilies
1 teaspoon lime juice or vinegar
salt and pepper to taste

Finely chop all vegetables and combine with remainder of ingredients. Chill.

Mango Chutney

Makes 12 6-ounce jars

This makes an excellent year-round gift.

1 quart	vinegar
3 pounds	brown sugar
4 pounds	half-ripe mangoes,* peeled and cubed
2 tablespoons	salt
2 pounds	raisins
1 ounce small	Hawaiian chili peppers* (6 – 8), seeded and minced
4 ounces	fresh ginger,* minced
4 ounces	garlic, minced

Boil vinegar and sugar for 5 minutes. Add mangoes and simmer until they are soft. Add remaining ingredients and simmer 1 to 1½ hours until fruit is glazed. Sterilize jelly jars, fill with chutney, and seal while hot with melted paraffin wax. Note: For milder chutney, use fewer chili peppers.

Chili Pepper Water

Makes 12 ounces

8 – 12 ounces	water
2 – 3 cloves	garlic, crushed
6 – 8	Hawaiian chili peppers,* mashed

Combine ingredients. Store in a jar and refrigerate.

Hot Pepper Jelly

Makes 1 quart

3 medium	sweet bell peppers
8 – 10	hot peppers
6^1/$_2$ cups	sugar
1^1/$_2$ cups	cider vinegar
1 bottle	Certo

Discard seeds and veins of peppers. Put sweet peppers and hot peppers through a meat grinder with a fine blade. Drain juice and pack peppers into 1 cup and use juice to flood to the full cup level. Bring sugar, peppers and vinegar to a hard boil. Set aside where it will keep hot for 15 to 20 minutes, stirring occasionally. Bring to a full boil again for 2 minutes and stir in Certo. Skim and stir repeatedly until slightly cool to keep peppers from floating. Pour in sterilized jars and seal.

Tarragon Mustard

Makes 2^1/$_2$ cups

This is sweet and hot.

4 ounces	dry mustard
^{5}/$_8$ cup	white vinegar
^{5}/$_8$ cup	tarragon vinegar
3	eggs
1^1/$_2$ cups	sugar
1 tablespoon	salt
1 tablespoon	dried tarragon

Combine dry mustard and vinegars in a blender. Beat eggs with sugar, salt and tarragon. Add vinegar-mustard mixture to eggs and cook over low heat until thickened. Cool. Pour into sterilized jars. Variation: Brown sugar may be substituted for the white sugar.

Green Mayonnaise

Makes 2¹/2 cups

Serve with crudités and seafood.

1 – 2 cloves	garlic
1 cup	parsley
4 – 5	green onions
¹/4 cup	chives
2	eggs or 3 egg yolks
2 – 3 tablespoons	lemon juice
1 tablespoon	Dijon mustard
¹/2 teaspoon	salt
	freshly ground pepper
1¹/2 cups	vegetable oil

Mince garlic, parsley, green onions and chives in a food processor. Add eggs, lemon juice, mustard, salt and pepper and process for 10 seconds. Pour oil through feed tube in a steady stream with motor running. Refrigerate to allow flavors to blend.

Compleat Kitchen
Honolulu, Hawaii

263

Mustard Mayonnaise
Makes 1 quart

1 quart	mayonnaise
2 tablespoons	Coleman's dry mustard
1/4 cup	horseradish
1/4 cup	lemon juice
3/4 teaspoon	salt

Mix all of the above ingredients together and refrigerate overnight before using.

Canlis' Restaurant
Honolulu, Hawaii

Papaya Pineapple Marmalade
Makes 2 1/2 quarts

Tasty on toast, a treat on vanilla ice cream.

10 cups	chopped firm-ripe papaya*
1 cup	shredded fresh pineapple
1	orange
2	lemons
3 tablespoons	grated fresh ginger*
1/2 teaspoon	salt
5 – 7 cups	sugar

Combine papaya and pineapple in large saucepan. Squeeze one cup of lemon-orange juice and grate all three citrus rinds. Add juice, grated rinds, ginger and salt. Bring to a boil and continue boiling (moderately) for 30 minutes. Add 5 cups sugar and taste for flavor. Add more if desired. Cook another 30 minutes, stirring frequently to avoid burning. Pour into sterilized jars. Note: Do not store longer than 6 months.

Tempura Batter

This is the Japanese version of batter-dipped, deep-fried shrimp and vegetables.

1	egg yolk
3/4 cup	ice water
1/4 teaspoon	baking soda
3/4 cup	flour
	oil for frying

Mix together egg yolk, ice water and baking soda. Sift flour into mixture. Stir lightly. Keep batter refrigerated until ready to use. Coat with batter and deep fry until golden brown. Note: The colder the batter, the lacier the tempura. You may want to drizzle a little batter around the edge of the food while it is frying for an extra lacy crunch.

Tempura* Sauce

1 cup	soup stock (dashi*)
1/3 cup	soy sauce
1/3 cup	mirin* or sake*
	finely grated daikon*

Combine first three ingredients and bring to a boil. Let guests add daikon to taste in individual serving bowls.

Glazing Oil

Makes 1 quart

One teaspoon glazing oil added to a stir-fry entrée while still in the wok* will enhance its flavor and appearance.

1 quart	vegetable oil
1/4 cup	fresh ginger* peelings
1/4 cup	sliced green onions
5	star anise*
5	Far chew spice* (optional)

Combine and simmer for 30 minutes. Strain and store in a cool place. Oil should keep 2 to 3 months.

Howard Co
Yen King
Honolulu Hawaii

Coconut Milk I

Makes 1 1/2 — 2 cups

1 fresh	coconut, peeled
	milk, water or coconut water*

Cut coconut into 1/2-inch cubes. For each cup of cubed coconut, add 3/4 cup of boiling liquid. Place in blender and process for 20 to 30 seconds on high speed. Let stand for 20 minutes. Strain through a double thickness of cheese cloth, squeezing out liquid.

Coconut Milk II

Makes 1 cup

1¹/3 cups   flaked coconut
1¹/3 cups   cold milk

Combine coconut and milk. Refrigerate for 1 hour. Place mixture in a blender and blend for 4 seconds. Strain.

Coconut Baked Bananas

Serves 6

This is an excellent side dish with curry as well as a tasty dessert.

1/4 cup   melted butter
6   firm bananas
2 tablespoons   orange juice
1/4 cup   brown sugar
1/4 teaspoon   cinnamon
1/8 teaspoon   nutmeg or mace
1/2 cup   shredded coconut

Preheat oven to 350 degrees. Roll bananas in butter, coating entire surface. Place in shallow baking dish. Sprinkle evenly with orange juice, brown sugar and spices. Bake for 10 minutes. Sprinkle with coconut and bake for 5 minutes longer. Watch that coconut does not burn.

Boiled Peanuts

Makes 1 pound

1 pound	raw peanuts in shell
1/2 cup	Hawaiian rock salt*
3 – 4	star anise*
1 teaspoon	sugar

Place peanuts in a pot and cover with water. Add rock salt, star anise and sugar. Bring to a boil, cover and simmer for 1 1/2 hours. Drain. Refrigerate. Note: If these appear to be too salty at first, let them sit before serving.

Green Chili Relish

Makes 2 quarts

Serve with crackers or chips. The longer this marinates, the better it is. It makes a nice gift.

3 (7-ounce) cans	diced green chilies, drained
3 (4 1/2-ounce) cans	chopped black olives
2 bunches	green onions, chopped
3 medium	tomatoes, peeled and chopped
1/2 cup	olive oil
1/2 cup	white wine vinegar
1/2 teaspoon	garlic salt

Mix green chilies and black olives. Add green onion and tomatoes. Mix olive oil, vinegar and garlic salt. Pour over first 4 ingredients. Store in refrigerator. Stir periodically.

Hilo
Pickled Mango

Makes 1 gallon

1 gallon	sliced green mangoes*
2 cups	raw sugar
1 cup	white vinegar
4 tablespoons	Hawaiian rock salt*
1/4 – 1/2 pound	seedless li hing mui*

Peel green mango with a vegetable peeler. Slice into thin strips and discard seed. Set aside. Bring sugar, vinegar and salt to a boil. Continue boiling until sugar dissolves. Cool. Stir in li hing mui and pour over mango slices. Store in airtight container. Note: Mangoes should be very small—3 to 4 inches in diameter. At this point you may cut through the seed. Common mangoes will give the best results.

Pickled
Maui Onions

Makes 1 gallon

1 quart	white vinegar
1 quart	water
1/3 cup	Hawaiian rock salt*
1/2 cup	sugar
4 pounds	Maui onions,* quartered
2 – 3	large carrots, sliced
1	large green pepper, sliced

Bring vinegar, water, salt and sugar to a boil. Pour over onions, carrots and green pepper. Let cool. Refrigerate 1 month.

269

Lime Baked Papayas

Serves 8

4	firm, ripe papayas*
4 tablespoons	lime juice
1/2 cup	melted butter
3/4 teaspoon	ground ginger
1/4 teaspoon	allspice
8	lime slices
dash	cayenne

Preheat oven to 350 degrees. Cut papayas in half length-wise and scoop out seeds. Arrange papayas in a glass baking dish with 1/8 inch warm water in the bottom. Mix lime juice, melted butter, ginger and allspice and divide among 8 papaya halves. Bake for 20 minutes, baste and bake another 10 minutes. Place a slice of lime at edge of each papaya half. Add a dash of cayenne and serve warm.

Seasoning Salt

Makes 30 ounces

1 (26-ounce) box	salt
2 – 4 tablespoons	cayenne
2 tablespoons	garlic powder
2 tablespoons	chili powder

Combine ingredients and store in a tightly covered container.

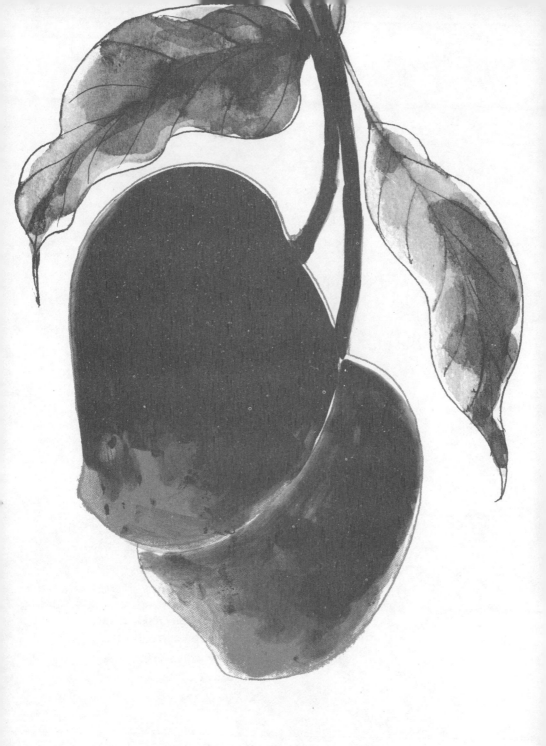

mango

Desserts

Desserts

Sauces

Brandied Hard Sauce 288

Grand Marnier Sauce 289

Macadamia Nut Parfait Sauce 288

Pineapple Brandy Sauce 289

Cakes

Angel Food Cake with
Butter Frosting 298

Banana Cake Waialae Iki 296

Bruce's Birthday Cake 295

Clem's Chocolate Cake 292

Coconut Cake 294

Guava Cake 293

Hawaiian Carrot Cake 299

Old Frame House Gingerbread 290

Patricia's Christmas Cake 297

White Chocolate Cake 291

Frostings

Butter Cream Frosting 298

Coconut Frosting 294

Cream Cheese Frosting 296

Fudge Frosting 292

Pies

"Never Fail" Pie Crust 300

Avocado Chiffon Pie 301

Macadamia Nut Pie 305

Magnolia Pie 300

Mango Pie 305

Pineapple Cream Cheese Pie 302

Pineapple Pie 303

Two Crust Banana Pie 304

Cookies

Caramel Cuts 308

Chinese Almond Cookies 309

Fragile Cookies 308

Garden Café Coconut Shortbread
Cookies 313

Glazed Almond Cookies 310

Haole Bars 312

Kalakaua Bars 311

Macadamia Nut Brownies 315

Oahu Ginger Snaps 307

O'Heneli Bars 314

Pecan Icebox Cookies 316

Regency Royals 306

Pineapple Dream Crêpes   *Serves 4*

8	crêpes (see index)
8 ounces	cream cheese, softened
1/3 cup	powdered sugar
1 (8-ounce) can	unsweetened pineapple, drained
1 cup	unsweetened pineapple juice
1/2 – 2/3 cup	sugar
1 tablespoon	cornstarch
2 tablespoons	butter
2 teaspoons	lemon juice
1 – 2 tablespoons	sherry

Garnish: Chopped macadamia nuts, whipped cream*

Mix cream cheese, powdered sugar and pineapple in a bowl. (You may want to add a small amount of water for a creamier texture.) Fill each crêpe with cream cheese mixture and fold. Combine pineapple juice, sugar and cornstarch in a double boiler over rapidly boiling water. After mixture thickens, remove from heat. Stir in butter and lemon juice. Cool. Flavor with sherry. When ready to serve, place 2 filled crêpes on dessert plate. Heat syrup topping and pour small amount over crêpes. Sprinkle with 1 tablespoon chopped nuts. Top with a dollop of whipped cream.

Fresh Strawberries No Ka Oi

Serves 6—8

No Ka Oi means the best, and you won't be disappointed.

3/4 cup	sugar
1/2 cup	whipping cream
1/4 cup	light corn syrup
2 tablespoons	butter
5 large	Heath bars, frozen
2 pints	fresh strawberries

Garnish: Sour cream

Combine sugar, whipping cream, corn syrup and butter in a saucepan. Bring to a boil and boil 2 minutes. Remove from heat. Chop frozen Heath bars into small pieces. (Bars may be placed in a plastic bag, then broken into bits with a hammer.) Stir in Heath bar bits to cooked mixture. Cool slightly. For each serving, place desired amount of strawberries into dessert bowl. Top with warm mixture and garnish with sour cream. Any left-over topping can be refrigerated, then reheated and thinned with cream.

Glazed Apple

Serves 2—4

The perfect finale to an Oriental meal.

1 cup	flour
1 cup	cornstarch
	water
1 pound	apples, peeled and cut into
	1-inch cubes
	vegetable oil

Mix flour, cornstarch and just enough water to make a thin solution. Dip apple cubes in mixture and deep fry in hot cooking oil until golden yellow. Drain.

Glaze

1 teaspoon	vegetable oil
1 tablespoon	water
1 cup	sugar
1 teaspoon	sesame seeds
1 teaspoon	water

Heat wok* for 10 seconds. Add oil, water and sugar. Stir quickly until sugar melts and turns into bubbling caramel syrup. Add deep-fried apples and then add sesame seeds. Toss until syrup covers each apple piece. Add 1 teaspoon of water to help crystalize the syrup and toss again. Transfer apple cubes one by one into a bowl of ice water to crystalize the syrup. Serve immediately. Variation: Bananas may also be used. Note: To flame the dessert, transfer apples from wok to well-oiled serving platter. Add a shot of brandy and ignite. Then transfer to ice water. Remove and serve.

Howard Co
Yen King Restaurant
Honolulu, Hawaii

Meringue aux Pommes   *Serves 6 – 8*

This dessert may be made in the morning and served for dinner.

6 – 7 large	green, firm cooking apples
$1/3$ cup	dry white wine
2 tablespoons	butter
	grated peel of 1 lemon
$1/2$ cup	red currant jelly

Peel and core apples. Slice into $1/4$-inch slices. In a 2-quart saucepan, cook apples in wine over low heat for 10 to 15 minutes. Shake pan occasionally so that apples do not stick. Do not overcook. Butter an 8-inch soufflé dish and spread apple slices over bottom. Sprinkle with grated lemon peel and dot with red currant jelly.

Meringue

6	egg whites
2 cups	sugar
1 teaspoon	vinegar
1 teaspoon	vanilla

Preheat oven to 275 degrees. Beat egg whites until soft peaks are formed. Gradually add sugar while beating. Add vinegar and vanilla. Continue beating for at least 8 minutes. Meringue will be shiny and form stiff peaks. Spoon meringue over apples, making a large, high swirl in the center and about a dozen ridges radiating out to the edge of te pan. Bake for 50 to 60 minutes. After 20 minutes, check meringue. If it is becoming dark, reduce heat to 250 degrees. Refrigerate if climate is humid.

Bambi's Flan *Serves 6*

$1/2$ cup sugar

Melt sugar in a saucepan over low heat until golden in color. Quickly pour into 8-inch round metal cake pan. Set aside. Note: Sugar will harden immediately.

8	eggs, separated
1 cup	sugar
3 cups	warm milk
1 teaspoon	vanilla
$1/2$ teaspoon	salt

Preheat oven to 350 degrees. Beat egg yolks in a large bowl until light in color. Slowly beat in sugar. Continue beating while gradually adding milk, vanilla, salt and egg whites. In order to remove all air bubbles, pour mixture through a fine strainer into the pan of hardened sugar. Set pan into a larger pan containing 1 inch of water. Bake for 1 hour or until knife comes out clean. Chill. Loosen sides and turn upside down onto a platter.

Michel's Grand Marnier Soufflé

Serves 8

1/4 pound	unsalted butter
2 1/2 cups	flour
3 1/4 cups	milk, warmed
8	egg yolks
4	whole eggs
1 cup	Grand Marnier
4	egg whites
1/2 cup	sugar
	powdered sugar

Preheat oven to 375 degrees. Heat the butter in a saucepan over moderate heat. Add the flour and stir until well blended. Add the warm milk and stir until very thick, making sure the mixture does not stick to the edge of the pan. Remove from heat, and beating constantly, add the egg yolks one by one. Continue beating while adding the whole eggs. Stir in the Grand Marnier. Beat egg whites until stiff. Continue beating while adding the sugar. Fold into the flour-egg mixture gently. Gently fold meringue into egg mixture. Butter individual soufflé dishes with unsalted butter and dust with flour. Fill dishes 3/4 full with batter and bake for 18 minutes. Remove from oven, dust with powdered sugar and serve immediately.

Michel's at the Colony Surf
Honolulu, Hawaii

Quick Cool
Lemon Soufflé

Serves 6

2 envelopes	unflavored gelatin
1/2 cup	water
6	eggs
11/2 cups	sugar
11/2 cups	heavy cream
1 tablespoon	grated lemon peel
2/3 cup	lemon juice

Garnish: Mint leaves

Prepare collar on a 1-quart soufflé dish. In a small sauce-pan, sprinkle gelatin over water and let soften for 10 minutes. Cook over low heat until gelatin dissolves. Cool. Combine eggs and sugar in a large bowl and beat at high speed until light. Whip cream and refrigerate. Combine grated lemon peel and juice with cooled gelatin and blend into egg-sugar mixture. Chill until mixture is thick enough to mound. Fold in whipped cream. Pour into soufflé dish and refrigerate 3 hours. Remove collar, garnish and serve.

Frosted Macadamia Nut Soufflé

Serves 8

```
1/2 gallon   macadamia nut ice cream
2 ounces     dark rum
             Garnish: Whipped cream, chopped
             macadamia nuts*
```

Line edge of eight 3-inch diameter ramekins with 1/4-inch waxpaper border. Mix ice cream with rum. Pour into ramekins. Freeze until solid. Before serving, remove border and garnish with whipped cream and a sprinkle of macadamia nuts.

Maile Restaurant
Kahala Hilton Hotel
Honolulu, Hawaii

Pele's Bananas

Serves 4

Madame Pele is the Hawaiian Goddess of Fire.

```
4 tablespoons   butter
6 tablespoons   brown sugar
1 teaspoon      cinnamon
4               bananas, sliced lengthwise
1/2 cup         banana liqueur
1/2 cup         rum
4 scoops        vanilla ice cream
```

Melt butter over low heat in a flambé pan or large skillet. Add sugar and cinnamon and mix well. Sauté bananas until they begin to turn soft. Add banana liqueur and half the rum and simmer. Bring remainder of rum to a boil in a separate saucepan. Quickly pour into flambé pan and ignite. When the flame dies, serve two slices of banana with a scoop of ice cream. Spoon remaining sauce over the ice cream.

Azuki Bean Sundae   *Serves 10*

A nice dessert to accompany a Japanese dinner.

1 can   azuki bean* paste
10 teaspoons   Midori Melon liqueur
1/2 gallon   vanilla ice cream

Place spoonful of azuki beans in a dessert dish. Scoop vanilla ice cream over beans. Top with 1 teaspoon liqueur. Serve with Senbei cookies.*

Strawberry Ice   *Serves 4*

Enjoy this as a sherbet, or as an accent to fresh fruit salads or desserts.

12 ounces   fresh strawberries
1   ripe banana
1   egg, beaten
1/2 cup   sugar
juice of 1 lemon

Hull and mash strawberries. Mash banana. Combine fruits with egg, sugar and lemon juice. Pour mixture into freezing tray and freeze for 1 hour or until half frozen. Stir the mixture, then return and freeze completely. Remove the ice from the freezer 15 minutes before serving. Note: If strawberries are not in season, use one 16-ounce package frozen strawberries and decrease sugar to 1/4 cup.

Old-Fashioned Strawberry Ice Cream

Makes 2 quarts

2	eggs
1¹/₄ cups	sugar
2 cups	Half and Half
¹/₄ teaspoon	vanilla
1 cup	whipping cream
3 cups	fresh strawberries, puréed

In a large bowl, beat eggs until thick and lemon colored. Add sugar, Half and Half, vanilla, and whipping cream. Stir in strawberries. Pour into ice cream canister. Freeze in ice cream maker according to manufacturer's instructions.

Mango Ice Cream

Makes 1 quart

³/₄ cup	sugar
1 tablespoon	lemon juice
¹/₄ teaspoon	salt
3 cups	whipping cream
1 cup	mashed mango*

Blend first 4 ingredients. Fold in mango. Pour into ice cream canister. Freeze according to manufacturer's instructions.

Coconut Mousse

Serves 10

Heavenly!

1 pint	Half and Half
3 envelopes	unflavored gelatin
1/3 cup	water
1 cup	sugar
2 cups	grated coconut
1 1/2 pints	whipping cream
1 teaspoon	coconut extract

In a saucepan, bring Half and Half to a boil. Dissolve gelatin in water. Add gelatin mixture and sugar, cooking until sugar dissolves. Cool and add coconut. Beat coconut extract and cream until stiff. Fold in whipped cream and pour into an 8-cup mold. Chill until firm.

Chocolate Mousse

Serves 8

3/4 cup	butter, softened
1 1/2 cups	sugar
1/2 teaspoon	almond extract
1 tablespoon	brandy
3	eggs, separated
1 cup	semi-sweet chocolate chips
1 cup	slivered almonds, toasted
2 cups	whipping cream, whipped
24 – 30	lady fingers, depending on size

In large mixing bowl, cream butter and sugar. Add almond extract, brandy and egg yolks. Melt chocolate chips in a double boiler. Remove from heat and add almonds to chocolate. Add chocolate mixture to butter mixture and blend well. Beat egg whites until stiff. Fold egg whites and whipped cream into mixture. Arrange lady fingers around sides of a spring form pan and pour in mousse. Chill several hours. Unmold and serve.

Grapes à la Crème

2 pounds	white seedless grapes
3/4 cup	sherry or brandy
1 pint	whipping cream
2 – 3 tablespoons	sugar
1/4 teaspoon	vanilla
1/2 pint	sour cream

Garnish: Brown sugar

Marinate grapes in sherry or brandy for 2 to 3 hours. Drain well. Whip the cream. Add sugar, vanilla and sour cream. Continue beating. Fold in grapes. Spoon into parfait glasses. Sprinkle brown sugar on top. Chill in the refrigerator for 6 hours or more.

Chocolate Cheesecake   *Serves 8 – 10*

Crust

3/4 cup	graham cracker crumbs
5 tablespoons	melted butter
2 tablespoons	sugar
2 tablespoons	grated semi-sweet chocolate

Combine ingredients and press firmly into the bottom of an 8 or 9-inch spring form pan. Chill while making filling.

Filling

3	eggs
1 cup	sugar
24 ounces	cream cheese, softened
12 (1-ounce) squares	semi-sweet chocolate, grated
1 cup	sour cream
3/4 cup	butter
1 teaspoon	vanilla
1 cup	chopped pecans
	Garnish: Whipped cream

Preheat oven to 325 degrees. Combine eggs and sugar and blend until light and creamy. Add softened cream cheese, blending until well mixed. In a double boiler combine chocolate, sour cream, butter and vanilla. Simmer until chocolate is melted. Stir chocolate mixture into cheese mixture. Fold in pecans. Pour into spring form pan and bake for 2 hours or until center is firm. Let cake cool on wire rack. Chill for 12 hours and serve with whipped cream.

Steamed Pudding

Serves 6—8

1/2 cup	butter
1 cup	sugar
1 cup	grated carrot
1 cup	grated potato
1 teaspoon	baking soda
1/2 teaspon	salt
1 cup	flour
2 tablespoons	powdered cocoa
1/2 teaspoon	nutmeg
1/2 teaspoon	cinnamon
1/8 teaspoon	ground cloves
1/3 cup	brandy or sherry
1/2 cup	chopped dates
1/2 cup	raisins

Lightly grease a small steam mold. Cream butter and sugar. Add grated carrot and potato. Sift dry ingredients and add to batter alternately with brandy. Stir in dates and raisins. Pour into steam mold and cover. Place steam mold in a large pot, resting on a tuna can with both ends removed. Fill pot with water to middle of steam mold. Cover pot and steam for 2 1/2 hours. May be wrapped in foil and frozen if baked ahead of time. Reheat in microwave. Serve with Brandied Hard Sauce (see index).

Brandied
Hard Sauce

Makes 1 1/2 cups

1/3 cup   butter, softened
1 cup   powdered sugar
pinch   salt
2 tablespoons   brandy

Combine ingredients, mixing well until creamy and smooth.

Macadamia Nut
Parfait Sauce

Makes 2 cups

Great over ice cream. Makes a lovely holiday gift.

1/3 cup   water
1/3 cup   brown sugar
1 cup   light corn syrup
1 cup   macadamia nut bits* or chopped
pecans

Bring water to a boil. Add sugar and dissolve. Add corn syrup and return mixture to a boil. Place nuts in a jar and pour in sugar mixture. Refrigerate until ready to serve. Sauce will thicken as it cools. Note: Sauce keeps well in the refrigerator.

Grand Marnier Sauce

Makes 1 1/2 cups

1 cup whipping cream
1/2 cup sugar
3 teaspoons lemon juice
7 tablespoons Grand Marnier
1 1/2 teaspoons grated orange peel

In a medium bowl, whip cream until soft peaks are formed. Fold in sugar, lemon juice, Grand Marnier and orange peel. Refrigerate. Serve with Grand Marnier Soufflé or fresh fruit.

Pineapple Brandy Sauce

Makes 1 cup

1 (8-ounce) can crushed pineapple, drained
1 tablespoon brandy
2 tablespoons brown sugar

Heat ingredients and serve with Two Crust Banana Pie (see index) or vanilla ice cream.

Old Frame House Gingerbread

Serves 12

This used to be served with mulled cider at the mission houses at Christmas time. In the evening, the houses were open and the Hawaiians sang traditional carols in their native tongue.

1 cup	sugar
1/2 teaspoon	salt
1 teaspoon	ground ginger
1/2 teaspoon	cinnamon
1/2 teaspoon	cloves
1 cup	vegetable oil
1 cup	molasses
2 teaspoons	baking soda
1 cup	boiling water
2 1/2 cups	flour
2	eggs, lightly beaten
	Garnish: Whipped cream or ice cream

Preheat oven to 350 degrees and lightly grease a 9 x 13-inch pan. Combine sugar and spices in a bowl. Stir in vegetable oil and molasses, mixing well. Add soda to boiling water and stir into mixture. Add flour, stirring to prevent lumps. Add eggs and mix well. Pour into greased pan and bake 40 to 45 minutes. Note: Hot coffee may be substituted for water.

White Chocolate Cake

1/2 pound	white chocolate, grated
1 cup	butter
2 cups	sugar
4	eggs, separated
2 1/2 cups	flour
1 teaspoon	baking powder
1/2 teaspoon	salt
1 cup	buttermilk
1 cup	chopped pecans
1 cup	flaked coconut
1 teaspoon	vanilla

Preheat oven to 325 degrees. In double boiler, melt chocolate and remove from heat. In a large bowl, cream butter and sugar until light and fluffy. Add egg yolks and beat well. Add chocolate. Sift flour, baking powder and salt together. Add to above mixture alternately with buttermilk. Mix well. Add pecans, coconut and vanilla. Beat egg whites until stiff and fold into batter. Pour into ungreased tube pan and bake for 1 hour and 10 minutes. Note: Do not allow water to come to a full boil when melting chocolate; steam changes chocolate consistency.

Clem's Chocolate Cake *Serves 16*

Chocoholics will enjoy the speed with which this rich cake can be prepared.

1/2 cup	margarine
4 heaping tablespoons	cocoa
1 cup	water
2 cups	flour
2 cups	sugar
1/2 cup	buttermilk
1 teaspoon	baking soda
2	eggs, lightly beaten
1 teaspoon	vanilla
1 teaspoon	cinnamon

Preheat oven to 425 degrees. Melt margarine in saucepan. Add cocoa and water and bring to a boil. Pour over flour and sugar. Combine buttermilk and soda and add with eggs, vanilla and cinnamon. Mix well and pour into a 9 x 13-inch pan. Bake for 20 minutes and frost immediately with Fudge Frosting.

Fudge Frosting

1/2 cup	margarine
4 tablespoons	cocoa
6 tablespoons	milk
1 (16-ounce) box	powdered sugar
1 teaspoon	vanilla
1 cup	chopped nuts

Combine margarine, cocoa and milk in saucepan and bring to a boil. Remove from heat and beat in sugar, vanilla and nuts. Pour over Clem's Chocolate Cake while hot.

Guava Cake

2 cups	sugar
1 cup	butter
4	eggs
3 cups	flour
3/4 teaspoon	nutmeg
1 1/4 teaspoons	baking soda
1/4 teaspoon	ground cloves
1/4 teaspoon	cinnamon
1 cup	frozen guava* juice concentrate
1/2 cup	guava juice
1/4 teaspoon	red food coloring

Preheat oven to 350 degrees. Cream sugar and butter until fluffy. Add eggs one at a time and beat well. Sift dry ingredients in a separate bowl. Mix guava concentrate and guava juice. Add dry ingredients and liquid alternately to creamy mixture until well blended. Pour into greased and floured 9 x 13 x 2-inch pan. Bake for 30 minutes. Cool and frost with Cream Cheese Frosting (see index) or Butter Cream Frosting (see index).

Coconut Cake

Serves 16

$^3/_4$ cup   butter
2 cups   sugar
$^3/_4$ cup   grated fresh coconut
2$^1/_2$ cups   flour
4 teaspoons   baking powder
1 cup   coconut water* (make up difference with milk)
4   egg whites

Preheat oven to 350 degrees. Butter and flour three 8-inch or two 9-inch round pans. Cream butter and sugar until light and fluffy. Add grated coconut. Sift flour and baking powder. Alternately add flour and coconut water to creamed mixture. Beat egg whites until they form soft peaks. Fold into batter. Pour batter into pans. Bake for 20 to 30 minutes. Top with Coconut Frosting.

Coconut Frosting

1 cup   sugar
$^1/_3$ cup   boiling water
$^1/_4$ teaspoon   cream of tartar
2 teaspoons   light corn syrup
2   egg whites
1 teaspoon   vanilla
2 cups   grated coconut

In a double boiler, mix sugar, water, cream of tartar and corn syrup. Stir until sugar dissolves. Add the egg whites and remove from heat. Beat mixture on high speed for exactly 5 minutes. Return to heat. Keep water simmering and heat mixture exactly 4 minutes longer. Add the vanilla. Frost each layer and sprinkle with coconut. Note: The frosting will keep in an airtight container in the refrigerator up to 1 week.

Bruce's Birthday Cake

This is a luscious pound cake.

1 cup	butter, softened
3 cups	sugar
6	eggs
1 cup	sour cream
3 cups	flour
1/4 teaspoon	baking powder
1 1/2 teaspoons	vanilla
	powdered sugar

Preheat oven to 350 degrees. In a large bowl, cream butter and sugar. Add eggs, beating well after each addition. Blend in sour cream. Sift flour, measure and sift again with the baking powder. Slowly add flour and vanilla. Pour batter into a buttered 9-inch bundt pan, an angel food cake pan or two 1-pound loaf pans. Bake for 1 hour 25 minutes or until done. Cool completely before sprinkling with sifted powdered sugar.

Banana Cake
Waialae Iki

1/4 cup	butter, softened
1 1/3 cups	sugar
2	eggs
1 teaspoon	vanilla
2 cups	flour
1 teaspoon	baking powder
1 teaspoon	baking soda
3/4 teaspoon	salt
1 (8-ounce) carton	sour cream
1 cup	mashed bananas
1 cup	chopped pecans

Preheat oven to 350 degrees. Grease and flour a 9 x 13-inch pan. Set aside. In a large mixing bowl, cream butter and sugar until light and fluffy. Add eggs and vanilla and blend thoroughly. Sift together flour, baking powder, baking soda and salt. Add to creamed mixture alternately with sour cream, beginning and ending with dry ingredients. Stir in bananas and pecans. Spread batter evenly over bottom of pan and bake 40 to 45 minutes. Cool and frost with Cream Cheese Frosting.

Cream Cheese Frosting

8 ounces	cream cheese, softened
1/4 cup	melted butter
1 teaspoon	vanilla
1 (16-ounce) box	powdered sugar

Combine all ingredients and blend well.

Patricia's Christmas Cake

Makes 2 1-pound loaves

1 cup	brown sugar
1 cup	sugar
2 cups	flour
1/2 teaspoon	salt
1/2 teaspoon	mace
1/2 teaspoon	nutmeg
1/2 teaspoon	allspice
1 teaspoon	baking soda
1 teaspoon	cinnamon
1/2 cup	vegetable oil
1 cup	buttermilk
3	eggs
1 cup	pitted prunes, diced
1 cup	chopped pecans

Preheat oven to 325 degrees. Sift dry ingredients into a large mixing bowl. Add oil, buttermilk, eggs and prunes. Beat 2 minutes. Add pecans. Bake in loaf pans for 1 hour or until done. Frost with Cream Cheese Frosting.

Angel Food Cake with Butter Cream Frosting

Serves 12

An elegant dessert when time is short.

1 (10-inch)	Angel Food cake

Butter Cream Frosting

1 cup	butter, softened
1/4 teaspoon	salt
2 1/2 cups	powdered sugar
5 tablespoons	whipping cream
1 teaspoon	vanilla

Combine butter, salt, powdered sugar and whipping cream. Beat with an electric mixter until very smooth and creamy. Stir in vanilla. Note: Additional powered sugar may be added to obtain desired consistency. Variations: Add 1 tablespoon instant coffee or cocoa and 2 to 3 tablespoons crème de cacao.

Hawaiian Carrot Cake

Serves 12 — 14

3	eggs
2 cups	sugar
1^1/$_2$ cups	vegetable oil
2 teaspoons	vanilla
1 (7-ounce) can	crushed pineapple, undrained
2 cups	grated carrots
3 cups	cake flour
^{1}/$_2$ teaspoon	allspice
1 teaspoon	baking powder
1 teaspoon	baking soda
1 teaspoon	salt
1 teaspoon	cinnamon
1 teaspoon	nutmeg
1 cup	chopped macadamia nuts*
1 tablespoon	powdered sugar

Preheat oven to 350 degrees. In a large mixing bowl, cream eggs, sugar and oil. Continue beating and add vanilla, crushed pineapple and carrots. Combine dry ingredients and sift 3 times. Slowly beat dry mixture into batter. Add nuts and blend thoroughly. Pour batter into greased and floured bundt pan. Bake for 1 hour and 15 minutes. While warm, dust with powdered sugar or cool and frost with Cream Cheese Frosting (see index).

"Never Fail" Pie Crust

Makes 2 9-inch crusts

1¼ cups	shortening
3 cups	flour
1	egg, beaten
5 tablespoons	water
1 tablespoon	white vinegar
1 teaspoon	salt

Cut shortening into flour. Mix egg with water, vinegar and salt. Add to flour mixture and blend well. Let dough rest 5 minutes. Roll out and trim to fit pie plate.

Magnolia Pie

Serves 8

Light and lemony.

1 (9-inch)	graham cracker crust
12 ounces	cream cheese, softened
2	eggs
²/3 cup	sugar
	grated peel and juice of ¹/2 lemon
1 cup	sour cream
3 tablespoons	sugar
	grated peel and juice of ¹/2 lemon

Preheat oven to 325 degrees. In a large mixing bowl, beat the cream cheese until smooth. Add eggs, sugar, lemon juice and grated peel. Beat until ingredients are well blended. Pour into crust and bake for 35 minutes. Cool. Combine sour cream, sugar and lemon juice and peel. Spread topping over pie. Cook an additional 5 minutes. Refrigerate 8 hours or overnight.

Avocado Chiffon Pie *Serves 8*

1 (9-inch)	pie shell, baked
1 cup	puréed avocado
3	egg yolks
1^1/$_2$ tablespoons	butter
^{1}/$_2$ teaspoon	nutmeg
1 teaspoon	cinnamon
^{1}/$_4$ cup	sugar
^{1}/$_2$ teaspoon	lemon juice
1 envelope	unflavored gelatin
^{1}/$_4$ cup	water
3	egg whites
^{1}/$_2$ cup	sugar
	Garnish: 1 cup whipping cream, whipped

Simmer avocado, egg yolks, butter, nutmeg, cinnamon, sugar and lemon juice for 10 minutes. Do not boil. Dissolve gelatin in water and add to hot mixture. Cool. Beat egg whites with sugar until stiff. Fold into the avocado mixture. Pour into baked pie shell. Chill for 8 hours or overnight. Garnish and serve.

Pineapple Cream Cheese Pie

Serves 8

1 (9-inch)	unbaked pie shell
1/3 cup	sugar
1 tablespoon	cornstarch
1 (9-ounce) can	crushed pineapple, undrained
8 ounces	cream cheese, softened
1/2 cup	sugar
1/2 teaspoon	salt
2	eggs
1/2 cup	milk
1/2 teaspoon	vanilla
1/4 cup	chopped pecans

Preheat oven to 400 degrees. Blend sugar with cornstarch and add pineapple. Cook, stirring constantly, until the mixture is thick and clear. Cool. Blend cream cheese with sugar and salt. Add eggs one at a time, stirring well after each addition. Blend in milk and vanilla. Spread the cooled pineapple mixture over the bottom of the pie shell. Pour in cream cheese mixture and sprinkle with pecans. Bake for 10 minutes, then reduce heat to 325 degrees and bake for an additional 50 minutes. Cool before serving.

Pineapple Pie *Serves 8*

Phyllo pie crust must be prepared just before adding filling.

Filling

2	eggs
2 teaspoons	lemon juice
1/3 cup	flour
1 cup	sugar
1/4 teaspoon	salt
2 cups	diced fresh pineapple

Beat eggs and lemon juice in a large bowl. Add flour, sugar and salt. Stir in pineapple with a wooden spoon. Set aside.

Crust

1 pound package	phyllo dough (16 sheets)
1/2 cup	melted butter (more if needed)

Preheat oven to 375 degrees. Lightly brush a 9-inch pie plate with melted butter. Fit one phyllo sheet into pan and brush lightly with butter. Continue to layer, brushing with butter, using 8 phyllo sheets. Pour in filling. Cover with 8 more phyllo sheets, brushing each with butter. Trim edges and flute. Bake for 30 minutes.

Two Crust Banana Pie

Serves 8

2 (9-inch)	unbaked pie shells
2$\frac{1}{2}$ cups	bananas, cut into $\frac{1}{4}$-inch slices
1 cup	pineapple juice
$\frac{1}{2}$ cup	sugar
3 tablespoons	flour
1 teaspoon	cinnamon
$\frac{1}{2}$ teaspoon	nutmeg
pinch	salt
1 tablespoon	butter
2 tablespoons	milk

Preheat oven to 400 degrees. Soak bananas in pineapple juice for 20 to 30 minutes. Drain. Combine dry ingredients and mix with bananas. Pour filling into pastry shell. Dot with butter and place top crust over filling. Seal and flute pastry edges, brush with milk and cut slits. Bake for 30 to 35 minutes. Serve warm or cold with Pineapple Brandy Sauce (see index).

Mango Pie

Hawaiian version of peach pie.

2 (8-inch)	unbaked pie shells
3 cups	peeled and sliced mangoes*
1/4 – 1/2 cup	sugar
2 tablespoons	flour
1/8 teaspoon	salt
1 1/2 tablespoons	lemon juice
1/2 teaspoon	cinnamon
1/4 teaspoon	nutmeg
1 tablespoon	butter

Preheat oven to 350 degrees. In large bowl, combine mangoes, sugar, flour, salt, lemon juice, cinnamon and nutmeg. Pour mixture into pie shell. Lattice strips of the second pie shell over top of pie and dot with butter. Bake for 1 hour. Note: Ripeness of mangoes will determine the amount of sugar needed. Use less sugar with riper mangoes.

Macadamia Nut Pie

1 (9-inch)	deep dish pie shell, unbaked
3	eggs
1 cup	sugar
1 1/2 tablespoons	flour
1/3 cup	melted butter
1 cup	dark corn syrup
1 1/3 cups	macadamia nut bits*
1 teaspoon	vanilla

Preheat oven to 400 degrees. Combine eggs, sugar, flour, butter, corn syrup, nuts and vanilla. Pour into pie shell and bake for 15 minutes. Reduce temperature to 350 degrees and bake until golden brown, an additional 40 to 45 minutes.

Regency Royals

Makes 2^1/$_2$ dozen

Crust

1 cup	sifted flour
^{1}/$_2$ cup	butter

Preheat oven to 375 degrees. Mix flour and butter. Press into a 9-inch square baking pan. Bake for 15 minutes.

Filling

2	eggs, slightly beaten
1^1/$_2$ cups	brown sugar, firmly packed
2 tablespoons	flour
^{1}/$_4$ teaspoon	baking powder
^{1}/$_2$ teaspoon	salt
1 teaspoon	vanilla
^{1}/$_2$ cup	shredded coconut
1 cup	chopped macadamia nuts*

In a bowl, combine eggs, sugar, flour, baking powder, salt and vanilla. Stir in coconut and nuts. Spread over warm crust and bake at 375 degrees for 20 minutes. When cool, ice with Orange-Lemon Frosting.

Orange-Lemon Frosting

2 tablespoons	butter, softened
2 cups	sifted powdered sugar
2 tablespoons	orange juice
1 teaspoon	lemon juice
^{1}/$_2$ cup	chopped macadamia nuts

Mix butter and sugar together. Add juices. Spread over Regency bars and sprinkle nuts on top.

Oahu Ginger Snaps   *Makes 4 dozen*

1/2 cup	butter
1/4 cup	vegetable shortening
1 cup	sugar
1/4 cup	molasses
1	egg, beaten
2 cups	flour
1 teaspoon	ground ginger
1 teaspoon	ground cloves
1 teaspoon	cinnamon
1/4 teaspoon	salt
2 teaspoons	baking soda.
	sugar

Preheat oven to 350 degrees. Cream butter, shortening and sugar. Add molasses and egg. Beat well. Add sifted dry ingredients, mixing well. Chill dough and roll into small balls. Dip in sugar and bake for 10 minutes. Note: Store in a tightly covered metal container to keep crisp.

Fragile Cookies

Makes 2 dozen

Meringue Chocolate Chip Cookies

3	egg whites
1/8 teaspoon	salt
1/8 teaspoon	cream of tartar
3/4 cup	sugar
6 ounces mini	semi-sweet chocolate chips
1/2 teaspoon	vanilla

Preheat oven to 300 degrees. Cover a cookie sheet with brown paper or a grocery bag. Beat egg whites until frothy. Add salt and cream of tartar. Add sugar 2 tablespoons at a time, beating until stiff. Fold in mini chocolate chips and vanilla. Drop from a teaspoon onto prepared cookie sheet. Bake for 30 minutes, then turn off oven and leave in for 45 minutes to one hour to dry. Store in tightly covered metal container. Note: Do not use recycled bags.

Caramel Cuts

Makes 3 dozen

A favorite with generations of Punahou students.

1/2 cup	melted butter
2 cups	brown sugar
2	eggs
2 cups	flour
2 teaspsoons	vanilla
2 teaspoons	baking powder
1/4 teaspoon	salt
	chopped nuts (optional)

Preheat oven to 350 degrees. Combine butter and sugar. Add other ingredients and mix well. Bake in greased 15 1/2 x 10 1/2 x 1-inch pan for about 25 minutes. Cool and cut into bars.

Chinese Almond Cookies

Makes 5 — 6 dozen

3 cups	sifted flour
4 tablespoons	finely chopped almonds
1 cup	sugar
1/2 teaspoon	salt
2 teaspoons	baking soda
1 1/2 cups	vegetable shortening
1	egg
1 teaspoon	almond extract
1 teaspoon	vanilla
	red food coloring

Preheat oven to 350 degrees. Mix dry ingredients and cut in shortening. Add egg, almond extract and vanilla and blend. Form a ball from a piece of dough the size of a quarter. Press the dough into a circle the size of a half dollar. Top each cookie with a dot of food coloring for good luck or whole or slivered almonds. Don't overhandle. Place on a greased cookie sheet 1/2-inch apart and bake for 12 minutes.

Glazed
Almond Cookies

This is a small cookie with a delicate almond flavor.

1 cup	butter, softened
1 cup	sugar
1/2 teaspoon	almond extract
1/2 teaspoon	vanilla
2	eggs, separated
3/4 cup	chopped blanched almonds
2 2/3 cups	sifted cake flour
1/2 teaspoon	salt
48	whole almonds

Preheat oven to 350 degrees. Cream butter and sugar until light. Beat in almond extract, vanilla and egg yolks. Add nuts, flour and salt. Mix well. Roll into 1-inch balls, dip into unbeaten egg whites and place 2 inches apart on greased cookie sheet. Put a whole almond in the center of each ball and push down to flatten cookie. Bake for 13 to 15 minutes.

Kalakaua Bars

Crust

1 cup	flour
3 tablespoons	powdered sugar
1/2 cup	melted butter

Preheat oven to 350 degrees. Mix flour, powdered sugar and butter. Press into an 8-inch square pan. Bake for 25 minutes.

Topping

2	eggs, slightly beaten
1 cup	sugar
1/4 cup	flour
1/2 teaspoon	baking powder
1/2 teaspoon	salt
1 teaspoon	vanilla
3/4 cup	chopped nuts
1/2 cup	shredded coconut
1/2 cup	maraschino cherries

Mix ingredients together. Pour over crust and bake 25 minutes. Cool and slice.

Haole Bars

1/2 cup	butter
1 cup	light brown sugar
1	egg
2 cups	chopped apples
1/2 cup	chopped walnuts
1/2 cup	flaked coconut
1/2 cup	raisins
1 cup	flour
1 teaspoon	salt
1 teaspoon	baking soda

Preheat oven to 375 degrees. Cream butter and sugar until light and beat in egg. Add apples, walnuts, coconut and raisins. Blend well. Sift flour, salt and baking soda and add to creamed mixture. Pour into a lightly greased 9 x 9-inch baking dish. Bake for 35 to 40 minutes.

Garden Café Coconut Shortbread Cookies

Makes 6 dozen

The Garden Café was founded in 1969. Excellent food and a pleasant atmosphere make lunching there a delightful experience.

3/4 pound	butter
1/4 pound	margarine
1 cup	sugar
1 teaspoon	vanilla
4 cups	flour
4 ounces	shredded coconut
	powdered sugar

Cream butter, margarine and sugar. Add vanilla and mix until fluffy. Add flour and coconut and mix well. Form dough into 3 long rolls and wrap individually in wax paper. Refrigerate for 8 hours or freeze for 2 hours. Preheat oven to 300 degrees. Slice dough 1/4-inch thick and bake on an ungreased cookie sheet for 25 to 30 minutes. Watch carefully and do not allow to brown. Cookies should be pale with just a hint of color. Cool on racks and sprinkle with powdered sugar.

Garden Café
Honolulu Academy of Arts
Honolulu, Hawaii

O'Heneli Bars

Bars

4 cups	oatmeal
1 cup	brown sugar
$^2/_3$ cup	melted butter
3 teaspoons	vanilla
$^1/_2$ cup	dark corn syrup

Preheat oven to 375 degrees. Mix ingredients. Spread into a greased 9 x 13-inch pan. Bake for 12 minutes. Cool for 30 minutes.

Frosting

1 (12-ounce) package	semi-sweet chocolate chips
$^2/_3$ cup	chunky peanut butter

Melt chips with peanut butter. Mix well. Spread on bars and refrigerate until frosting hardens.

Macadamia Nut Brownies

Makes 3 dozen

1¹/2 cups	sugar
²/3 cup	butter
¹/4 cup	water
1 (12-ounce) package	semi-sweet chocolate chips
2 teaspoons	vanilla
4	eggs, beaten
1¹/2 cups	flour
¹/2 teaspoon	baking soda
¹/2 teaspoon	salt
1 cup	chopped macadamia nuts*

Preheat oven to 350 degrees. Grease and lightly flour a 10 x 15-inch baking pan. In a large saucepan, combine sugar, butter and water, heating until sugar is dissolved and butter melted. Add chocolate chips and cook until melted. Stir in vanilla and set aside to cool. Add eggs to cooled chocolate mixture. Add flour, baking soda and salt, blending thoroughly. Fold in chopped nuts. Pour into pan and bake for 40 minutes. Cool and slice.

Pecan
Icebox Cookies

Makes 5 – 6 dozen

1 cup	butter
1/2 cup	brown sugar
1/2 cup	sugar
1	egg
1 teaspoon	vanilla
2 cups	flour
1/2 teaspoon	baking soda
1/4 teaspoon	salt
1/2 cup	chopped pecans

Cream butter and sugars. Add egg and vanilla. Sift dry ingredients and combine with creamed mixture. Stir in pecans. Roll and chill. Preheat oven to 350 degrees. Slice 1/4-inch thick and bake 8 to 10 minutes. Note: The thinner the slice, the crisper the cookie.

Plumeria

Lu'au

The Lu'au

A perfect expression of Hawaiian hospitality, the *'aha'aina or lu'au,* signifies a celebration of what the Hawaiian spirit and lifestyle are all about—an abundance of good food, laughter and music—shared with those you love.

Historically, the *lu'au* was a celebration to the gods giving thanks for having survived long and often arduous ocean voyages. It was a time of much feasting and praying, based on traditions from the homeland. Men and women ate separately and some of the foods were *kapu* (taboo) for the women to eat.

Through the years, the *lu'au* has become a traditional celebration of events such as a baby's first birthday, a wedding anniversary, a graduation or the completion of a project such as a new home or business. The celebration always begins with a prayer of thanks.

The size of a *lu'au* varies, but the most famous was given by King Kamehameha III on Restoration Day, July 31, 1843. It was estimated that 10,000 *kama'aina* (native-born or one adopting the Island spirit) and *malihini* (newcomers) attended the historical feast. The menu included "271 hogs, 482 large calabashes of poi, 662 chickens, 3 whole oxen, 2 barrels of salt pork, 3,125 salt fish, 1,820 fresh fish...4 barrels of onions, 180 squid"[1] and the event lasted around the clock.

[1] *Saga of the Sandwich Islands,* p. 520, Edward Scott, Sierra Tahoe Publishing Co., 1968.

The appropriate attire for a *lu'au* is one's best *aloha* shirt, *mu'umu'u* or *holoku* (long dresses). These are usually very colorful casual garments. Flower leis abound. Ladies wear flowers in their hair and *haku* (woven) head leis add to the tropical and festive atmosphere. Children are very much a part of the *lu'au* as there are always many aunties, uncles, *tutus* and *tutukanes* (grandmas and grandpas) to care for the little ones. Should one have an extra friend, the host usually says, "Of course, *hele mai* (come), bring him along. There's plenty!"

A musical group, usually comprised of ukulele, guitar, steel guitar and bass, welcomes arriving guests with favorite Hawaiian songs. Later, guests and family members offer graceful *hulas* (dances) and *mele hau'oli* (happy songs).

As the preparation and cost of a *lu'au* is considerable, family and friends usually *kokua* (help) and in doing so, demonstrate their *aloha* spirit (love). Some participants may gather *opihi* (limpet) off the rocks, catch fish and crabs and gather seaweed. Others may pick taro, bananas, sweet potatoes, flowers and *ti* leaves. Still others assist in preparation, cooking, serving and clean up. Overall, the organizing, decorating and execution of a *lu'au* is extensive.

The highlight of any *lu'au* is the *pua'a kalua* (pig) prepared in the *'imu* (underground oven). Although preparations commence the day before the *lu'au,* it is felt that the real beginning is the uncovering of the *'imu* and the emergence of the cooked pig, a fascinating ritual to watch.

Traditionally, Hawaiians sat on the ground on woven *lau hala* (Pandanus leaf) mats and ate the food with their hands from hand carved, polished wooden bowls. Today, one may see long low tables with pillows or grass for seats or standard height tables under large attractive tents or tarpaulins. Tables are usually covered with white butcher paper and adorned with long, shiny green *ti* leaves and masses of fresh plumeria, hibiscus and bougainvillea. A more formal setting may have round tables and linen tablecloths. A stage is placed just inside for entertainment and dancing.

A typical place setting may consist of a bowl of poi, a small condiment plate with *pipikaula* (beef jerky), Hawaiian rock salt, an Hawaiian chili pepper and a stalk of green onion. Another plate would consist of *poke* (raw seasoned seafood) *opihi,* raw crab and other seafood. Along-side rests a *ti*leaf with a piece of sweet potato, *haupia* (coconut pudding) or *kulolo* (taro pudding). Whole pineapples and coconut cake are placed in the middle of the tables about every fifth seat.

After the guests are seated, the main dishes are served in bowls or on wooden plates. These include: *lomilomi* salmon, chicken or squid *lu'au,* chicken long rice, *kalua* pig and *laulau.* Cold beer, mai tais and soft drinks accompany the feast.

Whether a lu'au for six hundred, or a *poi* supper for six, as long as flowers, music and food are plentiful, your lu'au will be a success.

Hele mai 'aha'aina.
Come join the feast.

Lu'au Menu

Kalua pig
Lomilomi salmon
Chicken or squid lu'au
Chicken long rice
Mullet Baked in Ti leaves
Poi
'Opihi
Raw black crab

Poke – aku or squid
Green onions with rock salt
Chili peppers
Pipikaula
Sweet potato
Haupia
Fresh pineapple
Cake

Poi Supper Menu

Laulau
Lomilomi salmon
Poi
Chicken long rice
or
Chicken lu'au

Haupia
Fresh pineapple
Cake
Any other variation of lu'au
dishes may be used

323

Kalua Pig

Depending on the size of the pua'a (pig), a suitable hole is dug in the ground. Hard wood is laid in the pit and is covered with river rounded lava rocks (which do not explode when heated). The wood is lit and the rocks are then heated for several hours until red hot. In the meantime, the pig is cleaned and the cavity rubbed with Hawaiian rock salt.* It is then placed on a large piece of chicken wire which is also used as a carrier. When the rocks are hot, some of them are placed in the cavity of the pig. The remaining rocks are covered with banana and ti leaves.* The pig is then lowered into the 'imu onto the bed of leaves. Bananas, sweet potatoes or fish pre-wrapped in ti leaves are then added. Everything is then covered with another heavy layer of banana and ti leaves which are topped with a heavy layer of wet burlap bags, and finally the loose dirt. It is then hosed down but NOT SOAKED. If any steam escapes during cooking, more dirt is added. For a 100 pound pig cooking time would be approximately 6 hours.

At the appointed time, the 'imu is uncovered and care is taken that no dirt is dropped on the food. The pig is now carefully lifted out by the wire mesh and the rocks are removed from its cavity by the very adept hands of the 'imu workers. They place their bare hands in a pail of cold water, reach in and remove each hot rock, toss it aside and redunk the hands to repeat the process. The pig is then carved and the meat shredded by hand.

Oven Kalua Pork
Serves 20

Oven Kalua Pork is a convenient substitute for pig from the 'imu. This is so easy and delicious you may want to serve it for a roast pork dinner.

8 pounds	pork butt
4 tablespoons	Hawaiian rock salt*
5 – 6 tablespoons	liquid smoke
6 – 8	ti leaves*

Preheat oven to 500 degrees. Rub rock salt and liquid smoke over pork. Wrap pork in leaves and then in heavy foil. Bake in covered pan for 1/2 hour. Reduce temperature to 325 degrees and cook for 3 1/2 hours. Shred into pieces and serve with a little of its own juice. Note: Banana leaves, taro leaves or spinach leaves may be substituted for a slightly different flavor.

Lomi Lomi Salmon
Serves 20

This is the salad at a poi supper or lu'au.

1 pound	salted salmon
4 pounds	tomatoes, finely chopped
2 medium	Maui onions,* finely chopped
1 cup	crushed ice
1 bunch	green onions, finely chopped

Soak salmon in water for 2 to 3 hours, changing water several times. Drain and remove skin, bones and white strings. Shred with spoon or fingers into small pieces. Place salmon, tomatoes and onions into a bowl. Refrigerate until well chilled. Top with thin layer of cracked ice one hour before serving. Just before serving, add green onions. Note: If unsalted salmon is used, rub salmon with rock salt and let stand overnight. Rinse completely and soak in water 1 hour or more, changing water 2 to 3 times.

325

Chicken or
Squid Lu'au

7	whole coconuts or 6 cups frozen coconut milk*
5 – 6 pounds	chicken thighs
or	
5 – 6 pounds	cooked squid
4 teaspoons	salt
6 cups	water
9 pounds	taro leaves*

Pierce eyes of coconuts, drain coconut water into a bowl and set aside. Crack coconut open, remove white meat and grate. Pour 4 cups of reserved coconut water (add tap water if necessary to equal 4 cups) over grated coconut meat and let stand 15 minutes. Squeeze coconut meat and juice through 2 thicknesses of wet cheese cloth into a bowl. Set aside. Place chicken in pot, add 3 teaspoons salt and 3 cups water and simmer uncovered until tender. Remove bones and cut chicken into 1-inch pieces and set aside. Cut squid in 1/2-inch pieces. Wash taro leaves, remove stem and strip tough part of rib. Place leaves, 3 cups water and 1 teaspoon salt in a deep saucepan. Simmer for 1 hour. Change water and cook 1 hour more until bitter "sting" is out of leaves. Squeeze out excess water. Add drained chicken or squid and coconut milk to cooked taro leaves. Heat thoroughly and serve immediately. Adjust flavor with additional salt.

Easy Chicken Lu'au *Serves 20*

Can be used as an easy recipe for chicken lu'au in place of taro leaves and fresh coconut.

16	chicken thighs
1 teaspoon	salt
6 pounds	frozen leaf spinach
2 (12-ounce) cans	frozen coconut milk*

Simmer chicken in salted water for 45 minutes or until tender. Bone, cut into bite-size pieces, and set aside. Thaw spinach, squeeze out excess water, add chicken and coconut milk. Heat until cooked through but do not boil. Serve hot.

Poi *Serves 20*

Poi is a starch that is made from the Taro plant. Although it may taste bland, poi takes on the flavor of the other foods.

7 pounds	poi*
1 – 2 cups	water

Use fresh, 1 or 2 day old poi. (Freeze-dried poi or bottled poi may be used although flavor is more bland.) Turn bag inside out and squeeze poi into a mixing bowl. Gradually add water, mixing and squeezing with hands until smooth. Consistency is like a thick paste. Cover bowl and keep in cool place. Serve at room temperature. Note: Each day it sits, it becomes more sour. If refrigerated, it will not sour as fast but must be covered with a layer of water. Mix with more water when ready to serve as poi will harden when cold.

Mullet Baked in Ti Leaves

Serves 20

4 pounds mullet*
¼ cup Hawaiian rock salt*
5 ti leaves*

Preheat oven to 350 degrees. Clean fish and sprinkle with salt. Lay fish lengthwise on a ti leaf. Wrap fish with additional leaves until covered. Tie ends with string or piece of stem. Place on jelly roll pan and bake uncovered for 30 to 40 minutes. Transfer to platter. Cut open ti leaves and serve. Note: Add onions if desired.

Green Onions with Rock Salt

Serves 20

*Delicious with poi.**

20 green onions
3 – 4 tablespoons Hawaiian rock salt*
Hawaiian chili pepper* (optional)

Trim onions until each is about 6—8 inches long with white lower stem and some green top. Serve on square of ti leaf with ½—1 teaspoon rock salt on the side for "dipping." A fresh small Hawaiian chili pepper may also be served. Note: Save remaining onion tops for use in Lomi Lomi Salmon (see index).

Chicken
with Long Rice

This can be served as a main dish with steaming hot rice.

5 pounds	chicken thighs
12 cups	water
1 – 2 inches	fresh ginger,* crushed
2 tablespoons	Hawaiian rock salt*
2 cloves	garlic, crushed (optional)
20 ounces	long rice*
1 bunch	green onions, chopped

Garnish: Chopped green onions

Cover chicken with water. Add ginger, half the rock salt and garlic and simmer 45 minutes or until tender. Cool. Bone chicken and cut into bite-size pieces. Reserve broth. Remove ginger and discard. Add long rice to reserved broth and let stand 1/2 hour. Remove long rice and cut into 4-inch lengths. Return long rice to broth. Add green onions, remaining rock salt and chicken. Bring to boil and simmer 15 to 20 minutes. Add additional salt if desired. Chicken long rice will be moist with a bit of broth as a sauce. Garnish with chopped onion. Note: If made the day ahead, add a little extra chicken broth before reheating as the long rice will absorb existing broth.

Laulau
Makes 20

A delicious neatly wrapped bundle of pork, beef and fish wrapped in taro and ti leaves and served in place of kalua pig at a poi supper or lu'au.

1¹/₂ pounds	salted butterfish* or salted salmon
2¹/₂ pounds	beef brisket or bottom round
5 pounds	pork butt
2 pounds	pork belly (optional)
200	taro leaves,* (10 per laulau)
60	ti leaves,* (3 per laulau)

Salted fish should be soaked for ¹/₂ hour before cutting, changing the water twice. Cut fish and beef into 1-inch cubes and pork into 1¹/₂—2-inch cubes. Set aside. Wash ti and taro leaves. Remove tough ribs from the back of all leaves with small sharp knife. Remove stems from taro leaves. Peeled taro leaf stems may be cooked in laulau. Set ti leaves aside.

Assemble each laulau as follows: Place 10 taro leaves in a stack. In the middle of each place a piece of fish, beef, pork and pork belly. Fold leaves to middle to make a neatly wrapped bundle.

Place 2 ti leaves across each other to make an "X." Place taro bundle on "X" with folded side down. Bring ends of one ti leaf together, closing tightly over bundle with ends standing up. Bring ends of second ti leaf together in the same way. Place bundle on a third ti leaf and close in same manner to ensure total coverage of the bundle. Stems and ends should all be standing up. Holding bundle tightly with one hand, split stem of third ti leaf into two lengths with other hand. This will be your tie. Wind stem ties around the stems and ends several times, securing tightly and finish with a knot. Cut remaining stems and ends 3 to 4 inches above knot for a neat package.

Steam laulau for a minimum of 4 hours.

Pipikaula

Pipikaula * *is Hawaiian beef jerky.*

4 pounds	flank steak or brisket
1/3 cup	red Hawaiian salt * or rock salt
1/4 cup	water
1/2 cup	soy sauce
2 tablespoons	brown sugar
2 cloves	garlic, minced
1 tablespoon	vegetable oil
	soy sauce

Slice meat across the grain 1/4 inch thick and 6 to 8 inches long. Sprinkle with salt. Drizzle with water and let stand for 1 hour. Mix soy sauce, brown sugar, garlic and oil. Marinate meat overnight. Lay meat slices on a rack over a baking pan. Dry the meat in hot sun for one day, turning occasionally. Brown meat over a charcoal fire or fry in a pan in oil. Drizzle meat with soy sauce and serve.

Poke Aku

Serves 20

A fresh raw fish flavored with seaweed and kukui nut (inamóna) which is served as a side dish or a pupu.

5 pounds	fresh aku*
3 pounds	chopped limu koho* or manuea*
	Hawaiian rock salt* to taste
3 – 4 tablespoons	inamóna*

Skin the fish and cut into 1-inch cubes. Combine with remaining ingredients. Chill and serve. Note: Fresh swordfish squid or octopus may be substituted. Must be fresh. Variation: Korean style poke may be made using 3—5 seeded chopped Hawaiian chili peppers,* 1 bunch chopped green onions, 2 tablespoons toasted sesame seeds, 1 tablespoon sesame oil* and 2 tablespoons soy sauce. Adjust to taste.

Haupia

Serves 20

Traditional dessert served with Lu'au food.

12 ounces	frozen coconut milk*
1 1/2 cups	water
1/2 cup plus 2 tablespoons	sugar
1/2 cup plus 2 tablespoons	cornstarch

Combine all ingredients in saucepan. Stir over medium heat until thickened. Lower heat and cook for ten minutes, stirring constantly to avoid lumping or burning. Pour into 8 x 8-inch dish and chill until set. Cut haupia* into squares. Note: May be topped with crushed pineapple, sliced peaches or sliced mango.

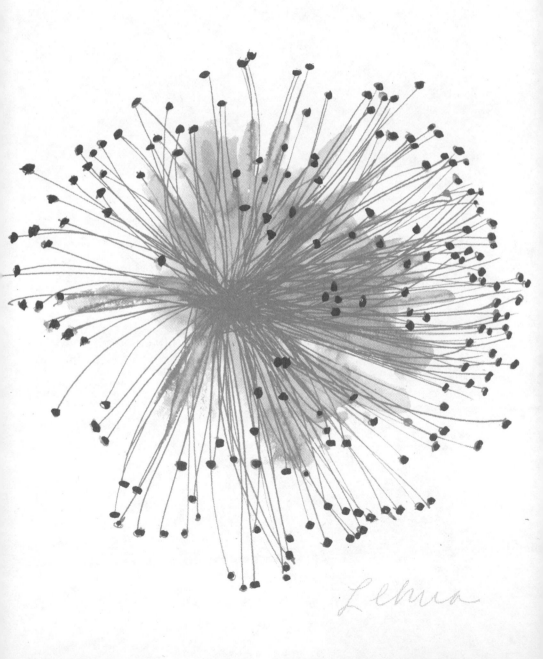

Lehua

Hawaiian Fish and Seafood Chart

By Margo Stahl, Marine Biologist

Fish have long been recognized as having unique nutritional as well as a cosmopolitan gustatory appeal. Although some oily fish suffer from the stigma of being "fishy," most fish contain less than 5% fat. This fat has remarkable food value. Not only do fish contain high proportions of polyunsaturated fatty acids, they also contain relatively small amounts of cholesterol. Consequently, fish and shellfish are frequently recommended for those individuals seeking more healthful diets.

Hawaii has many delectable species of fish and shellfish. This chart will introduce you to some of the local favorites.

Tunas

Tunas are the commercially most important group of fishes in Hawaii. Their silvery bodies can range in size up to several hundred pounds. They are marked with dark areas on top and light undersides; this countershading allows them to blend in with their environment. Good table quality tuna flesh has a translucent rosy to red color. The older and bigger the fish, the deeper the hue of the flesh. They are usually bought in fillets. Sashimi, raw tuna, is an Island delicacy. Cooking tends to make the taste and smell of tuna more pronounced.

Aku, Skipjack Tuna, Ocean Bonito, Katsuo

Aku is canned for export. When eaten raw, as sashimi, it has a surprisingly delicate flavor. Try baking a whole small aku, basted in soy sauce and liquid smoke and wrapped in foil.

Ahi, Yellowfin Tuna, Shibi
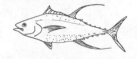
Ahi flesh is lighter in color than aku. Raw ahi is an excellent choice for sashimi or it may be sauteed in sesame oil with soy sauce, chili peppers and green onions.

Ahipalaha, Albacore, Tonbo

Albacore tuna have the whitest flesh of any of the
tunas and frequently command a high price. Peak
landings are in the summer and most fish are
very large.

Billfish

A'u, Pacific Blue Marlin, Kajiki

The blue marlin is presently the most important
Hawaiian billfish, both from the commercial and
recreational standpoint. This fish travels the Atlantic,
Pacific, and Indian oceans and is highly prized
everywhere. However, billfishes are not of major
commercial significance on the mainland as they are
here in Hawaii and are frequently wasted as by-
catches of recreational tournaments there. Marlin
steaks are delicious barbequed or broiled. Look for
them in the markets during the summer months.

A'u, Striped Marlin, Naraigi

This species is the next most important billfish
in the Hawaiian markets and is found throughout
the Indo-Pacific region. It is similar to the blue
marlin and can be found as steaks or fillets along-
side blue marlin during the summer months.

A'u, Broadbill Swordfish

Found throughout the world, the controversial
federal ban on swordfish reported to contain high
levels of mercury has done little to discourage its
popularity and high market prices. It is usually
sold in fresh or frozen inch-thick steaks during the
summer and fall months. The meat is firm and of
distinctive flavor. It is best either oven broiled
or charcoaled.

Snappers

There are many taste-tempting snappers found in Hawaiian waters. The
Penguin Bank-North Molokai region and the remote Northwestern Hawaiian
Islands are prime fishing grounds. Snappers are usually brightly colored with
red and yellow hues. The flesh of the snapper is white, firm yet tender, charac-
teristically mild, and tasteful. The holiday season brings the greatest demand,
accompanied by higher prices.

Opakapaka

An Island favorite, this pink snapper is usually available from 2 to 12 pounds. It is delicious baked, fried, broiled or as sashimi. Catches of opakapaka are greatest in December.

Kalekale

This pinkish fish is a prized addition to any table. It can frequently be purchased from 1 to 4 pounds.

Onaga

This beautiful red fish is ranked near the top for taste among the snappers. Locally this red snapper can reach a size of 36 pounds, but more often, it will range from 1 to 15 pounds. It is available in the markets particularly around New Year's.

Ehu

This large-eyed fish may weigh up to 12 pounds, but it is commonly purchased between 1 and 5 pounds. Like its relative, the onaga, it is caught at depths of 600 to 1000 feet. Ehu is available year round, with greatest supplies in December.

Uku

This gray snapper has mean-looking canine teeth and averages 7 to 8 pounds. It can reach up to 50 pounds, however. Unlike the other snappers, it is more available in the summer.

Taape

This snapper is yellow. Recently, young taape were deliberately introduced into our waters. The introduction was quite successful and now they are very abundant in the market at reasonable prices year round. Size ranges from 1/2 to 1 pound, making them an ideal size for pan frying.

Grouper

Hapuupuu

This is the only grouper of any major commercial significance in Hawaii. It is a white, firm fleshed fish, ranging in size up to 50 pounds. Delicious baked or cubed and stir-fried with vegetables. Maximum landings of this fish are in September, but it can be purchased year round.

Jacks

Ulua, Papio

Ulua refers to any one of eleven different species
of large Jacks. The white ulua is slightly higher
priced than the black. They all have a firm, white
flakey flesh. The silver ulua and pig ulua are also
delicious. Papio are the young of the several
species of ulua and refer to ulua under 10 pounds.
They are delicious pan-fried. The head is excellent
as the basis for fish chowder. Available most of
the year.

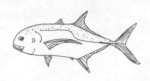

Akule, Hahalalu, Pa'a'a, Big-Eyed Scad, Aji

This large eyed, mackerel-looking fish is oilier with
more dark muscle area. The dark muscle is more
flavorful, like light and dark meat in chicken. The
fish is moist, with a coarse texture. Try them fried,
baked, smoked or dried. They are especially available
from February through August.

Opelu, Mackerel Scad

This fish is similar to akule. It is considered "fishy"
by some. It is delicious dried and smoked. Look for
this fish in the fall.

High Seas Fish

Mahimahi, Dolphinfish, Mansaku

A large fish with delicate firm white flesh. It is
available fresh in fish markets, though most of our
frozen mahimahi is imported. The price varies greatly
between fresh and frozen fish. Mahimahi is frequently featured in local restaurants. It is especially
popular fried in egg batter. The dolphinfish is not
to be confused with the porpoise. It is available
here year round. It can also be found on the East
and West coasts although it is not as popular.

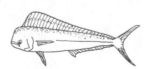

Ono, Wahoo, Sawara

Ono has a very moist, slightly coarse white flesh
(not quite as firm as mahimahi). The fish averages
40 to 100 pounds, therefore it is usually purchased
as ono steaks rather than whole. Excellent broiled
or sauteed. Available year round.

Nearshore Fish

Kumu, Goatfish
This fish is red in color and has firm white flesh. It can reach 6-9 pounds, however, it is frequently available in smaller sizes, from ½ to 3½ pounds. Steamed Kumu is an Island specialty. Available year round.

Mullet
There are several species of mullet in Hawaiian waters, although most restaurants import it for their menu. Island raised pond mullet are also available. The average weight is 1½ pounds. For a taste treat steam mullet with ginger and green onions. It is obtainable year round.

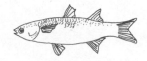

Shellfish

Lobster
Local lobster tails come from the Northwestern Hawaiian Islands. Depending on the weather, they are available year round.

Shrimp
We are fortunate to have delicious marine shrimp, some of which are caught in very deep water. This expanding fishery is providing fresh and frozen shrimp to numerous local restaurants. As this fishery is developed, availability will increase.

Hawaiian Freshwater Prawn
Freshwater prawns are an important part of Hawaii's expanding aquaculture industry. These delicately flavored prawns taste great in garlic butter and ginger. Available year round.

Hono Hono
Orchids

Glossary

Ahi
(See fish chart)

Aku
(See fish chart)

Azuki Beans, Azuki Bean Paste
Small red beans frequently used in Japanese cooking. They are often boiled with sugar to make a sweet red bean paste (an) which is then used in Japanese confections. The paste is made in two textures: smooth (koshi-an) and chunky with beans partially crushed (tsubushi-an).

Bean Sprouts
Sprouted mung beans. Available in markets and health food stores, fresh or canned. Can be sprouted from seeds.

Black Chinese Mushrooms
These rather expensive dried mushrooms have a distinctive meaty flavor. To prepare, place in water to cover, soak until soft (about 15 minutes) and discard stems.

Breadfruit
Large melon-size starchy fruit that can be eaten either half ripe or very ripe. The ripe stage should be baked and flavored like a yam or sliced thinly and deep-fried. The half ripe stage is peeled and steamed or boiled. Can be used instead of potatoes in a stew.

Butterfish

Black cod, a high fat, strongly flavored fish used in Japanese cuisine. May substitute bluefish, sheepshead or other oily fish.

Char Siu

Marinated pork that is reddish pink in color and has a sweet spicy flavor. The meat is usually roasted or barbecued. Char siu is often added to stir-fry dishes.

Chicken Lu'au

Chicken cooked with coconut milk and taro or spinach leaves.

Chili Oil

Oil flavored with hot chilies. It is used as a seasoning in many Chinese dishes. It has a shelf life of approximately 6 months. Keeps its flavor longer if refrigerated.

Chinese Five Spice

This unusual seasoning contains star anise, anise pepper, fennel, cloves and cinnamon in varying quantities. The Chinese name is Ng Heong Fun.

Chinese Black Beans, Chinese Black Bean Paste

Fermented black soy beans preserved in salt. They are also mashed and made into a paste or sauce. Both are used as seasoning for meats, fish and poultry.

Chinese Parsley

A coriander spice plant which is also known as cilantro. The strong flavor of the leaves is important in Chinese and other Asian cooking.

Chinese Peas

Also known as Snow Peas or Sugar Peas, they are light green and crisp. The entire pod is edible and may be found frozen or fresh. To prepare, remove strings.

Choi Sum

Tender, delicately flavored center of bok choy, one of several Oriental cabbages.

Chow Fun Noodles
Wide, flat noodles made of rice, cooked and mixed with meat and vegetables in Chinese dishes.

Chutney
A spicy relish made with fruits, spices and herbs. Usually served with curry.

Cilantro
(See Chinese Parsley)

Cloud Ears
A dried fungus with no real flavor of its own. The somewhat crunchy consistency and the dark color add interest to a variety of Asian dishes. When soaked in water, it expands to 5 times its size.

Coconut
The nut or fruit of a coconut palm. Meat of young coconut can be spooned. The mature coconut is usually grated. Shredded and flaked coconut is available in cans or packages.

Coconut Milk
The creamy liquid extracted from the grated flesh of fresh coconut. The flavor is unique. Coconut milk is available frozen.

Coconut Syrup
Coconut syrup is made from coconut water, grated fresh coconut, sugar and cream of tartar.

Coconut Water
The liquid found in the center of a coconut. There are 3 eyes on the top of the coconut which can be opened to drain the liquid.

Creole Mustard
A distinctive mustard made in the New Orleans area. Available in many gourmet food sections.

Crystalized Ginger

Crystalized ginger, also known as candied ginger, is often used in desserts.

Cuttlefish

Similar to squid (calamari). Available fresh, frozen and dried.

Da Kine

Catch-all phrase for miscellaneous items.

Daikon

A common ingredient in Japanese cooking. It is in the turnip family though it is more radish-like in flavor. Any turnip may be used as a substitute.

Dashi

A stock based on dried bonito and kelp, similar to bouillon.

Dried Red Curry Stock

A powder made from dried red chili, spices, coconut cream and salt. Identified with Thai cooking.

Fall Pine Mushrooms

Also called Matsutake. They are available fresh or canned, but never dried. They have a distinctive texture, woodsy fragrance and add a unique flavor to soups and poultry.

Far Chew Spice

Szechuan peppercorns often combined with salt to make a table seasoning.

Fish Cake

Also known as Kamaboko, this is a puréed steamed loaf of whitefish. The outer surface is sometimes tinted bright pink. Can be deep-fried, broiled or steamed.

Fish Paste

A gel made by scraping raw white fish and blending with salt and water. Awa (milk fish) or oio (bonefish) may be used.

Furikake

Seasoning for rice and noodles containing seaweed, sesame seeds and salt. Adds color and flavor.

Ginger

A gnarled light brown root with a pungent, spicy flavor. Garlic and ginger are the basic flavors in many stir-fry dishes. Peel and slice, mince or grate for maximum flavor. The Japanese use a special ginger grater with fine teeth to make a fresh paste. Ginger juice may be obtained by squeezing a small chunk of ginger in a garlic press. To store, refrigerate in a jar of sherry or freeze in a plastic bag.

Ginger Slivers

(See Ginger)

Guava

Tropical fruit the size of an apricot or plum with a unique flavor. The entire cavity of the fruit is comprised of seed. It is used primarily in juice, preserves, jellies, sauces and syrups or eaten raw. It is readily available in Hawaii, California, and Florida. Canned guava shells can be purchased in the gourmet section of markets or specialty shops.

Hana Ebi

Dried shredded shrimp. Available in green and red, it is used for color as well as flavor. Available in the Oriental section of most markets.

Hana Katsuo

Dried shaved bonito flakes that resemble rose colored wood shavings. Sold in cellophane packages.

Haupia

Coconut pudding eaten as a dessert.

Hawaiian Chili Pepper

A small, attractive orange-red fruit used as a spicy seasoning.

Hawaiian Rock Salt
Salt used for cooking. It is available in white and red, which has been colored with clay. Coarse salt or kosher salt can be substituted.

Hoisin Sauce
Fermented bean sauce that is sweet and pungent. Made from soy beans with garlic, glutenous red rice, salt and sugar. It is used as a condiment with dishes such as pork or roast duck and is often an ingredient in a marinade for poultry.

Inamona
Kukui nut paste used for flavoring in poke or as a condiment for other lu'au dishes.

Kalbi
Beef short ribs marinated in a Korean sauce with a soy sauce and sesame base.

Kamaboko
(See Fish Cake)

Kim Chee
Korean pickled cabbage served as a relish. Includes onions, radishes, garlic and chilies. Sold in refrigerated section of grocery stores.

Ko Choo Jang
A Korean seasoning of powdered chili peppers mixed with mochi, rice, water, miso, honey and salt. It must be refrigerated.

Konbu
Dried folded sheets of kelp. Do not wash. Gently wipe away any surface powders. Score lightly to release flavor.

Kūlolo
Steamed taro pudding eaten as a dessert.

Kumu
(See fish chart)

Kwo Pee
Dried orange peel. Also spelled gwoh pay.

Laulau
Steamed bundle of pork, fish and beef wrapped in taro or spinach leaves and enclosed in ti leaves.

Li Hing Mui
Preserved plum with or without the seed. It has a sweet, salty, licorice flavor.

Limu Kohu
A soft, succulent, small red seaweed used in raw fish dishes.

Lomi Lomi Salmon
A chilled fish dish of salted salmon, onions, green onions, and tomatoes. Traditionally served at luaus.

Long Rice
Dried bean curd thread-like noodles. Made from mung bean flour. Must be soaked in water before cooking to absorb flavor of food with which they are cooked.

Lumpia
A Filipino appetizer similar to a spring roll.

Lumpia Wrapper
A rectangular shaped pastry used to wrap around a meat filling. Size and shape distinguish it from a won ton pi.

Lup Cheong Sausage
Chinese sausage flavored with anise. It is slightly sweet with a licorice flavor and very fatty.

Lychee
A traditional Chinese fruit with a woody exterior around a sweet fleshy white flavored pulp. Fresh lychee may be frozen. Canned lychee is peeled and often seeded.

Macadamia Nuts

A member of the protea family, this nut is a delicacy. Can be purchased whole, in pieces or in bits. For cooking, unsalted nuts are preferred. Macadamia nuts freeze very well.

Mahimahi

(See fish chart)

Malasada

Portuguese doughnut.

Mango

A tropical yellow-pink fruit with bright orange flesh. Has a high fiber content. Best known varieties are Haden, Pirie and Gouveia. A ripe mango is slightly soft and has a strong fragrance.

Manoa Lettuce

A leafy, semi-head lettuce also known as Green Mignonette. Any leafy green lettuce may be substituted.

Maui Onion

A sweet, and mild onion. It is a Texas Bermuda Granex Grano type onion grown in volcanic soil. A Texas onion or a Vidalia sweet onion can be substituted.

Mirin

Heavily sweetened rice wine used for flavoring or in marinades, it is an important ingredient in Japanese cooking. One teaspoon of sugar may be substituted for 1 tablespoon of mirin.

Miso

A fermented soy paste used in soups and stews. Aka miso is a dark red strongly flavored miso and shiro miso is a white, sweet, mildly flavored miso.

Mochi Rice

Glutenous rice.

Mullet

(See fish chart)

Namasu

A Japanese salad made of raw vegetables marinated in a rice vinegar dressing.

Nori

Thin sheets of dark green or purplish dry seaweed used to wrap sushi or mochi (rice balls), adding color and a distinctive taste to the rice. Most commonly available in cellophane packages, usually 10 sheets to a package. It may also be available in canisters or tin boxes.

Onaga

(See fish chart)

Ono

(See fish chart)

Opakapaka

(See fish chart)

Opihi

Small shell limpets found on ocean rocks. May substitute small mollusks such as clams or mussels.

Oyster Sauce

Spiced concentrated liquid in which oysters have been cooked.

Panko

A Japanese crispy flour meal used for breading. Similar to coarse white bread crumbs.

Papaya

A pear or light-bulb shaped yellow fruit with melon-like flesh.

Papio

(See fish chart)

Passion Fruit

A plum-size fruit with a tangy citrus-like taste. Juice is extracted and used as a flavoring. It is available as a frozen concentrate. Also called lilikoi.

Pickled Ginger
Baby ginger that has been pickled in sweet vinegar and then either slivered or sliced. It is used as a garnish or palate refresher. It comes in red or pink.

Pipikaula
Hawaiian beef jerky. It is cured dried beef.

Poi
Steamed taro root pounded into a thick paste.

Poke
Fresh raw fish mixed with seaweed, kukui nut paste, hot red peppers, sesame seeds or any other combination to make a fish salad.

Portuguese Sausage
Highly seasoned pork sausage. Red pepper is liberally used in this sausage. It is available mild or hot. Spicy Italian sausage may be substituted.

Pua'a Kalua
Roasted pig.

Pupu
Finger food. Literally, a relish, snack or hors d'oeuvre.

Rice Flour
Made from steamed glutenous rice. Used for dumplings and confections, as well as a thickener for sauces.

Rice Vinegar
Vinegar made from fermented rice. It is lighter and sweeter than most Western vinegars. It is also called Japanese rice vinegar or Tamanoe vinegar.

Rice Wine
A Japanese wine known as sake, which is used in cooking and as a beverage. Dry sherry may be substituted.

Sake
Japanese rice wine with a low alcohol content. It is fragrant and colorless.

Sashimi
Fresh, thinly sliced, uncooked salt water fish.

Senbei Cookies
Japanese rice wafers with a variety of flavorings: miso, coconut, sesame seed, ginger and soy sauce. The most familiar is the traditional fortune cookie.

Sesame Oil
Oil pressed from the sesame seed. Highly concentrated and very flavorful. It is especially prevalent in Korean and Chinese cooking.

Shiitake
Dried, brown mushrooms served as a condiment, a separate course or with rice. Mushrooms are soaked to desired texture.

Simple Syrup
A syrup made by dissolving sugar in an equal amount of boiling water.

Snow Peas
(See Chinese Peas)

Somen Noodles
Thin fine round white Japanese noodles that cook quickly. They are shorter and thinner than spaghetti noodles.

Soy Sauce
A liquid made of soy beans, barley and salt used as the principal seasoning in Oriental cooking. Also known as shoyu.

Squid Lu'au
Squid cooked with coconut milk and taro or spinach leaves.

Star Anise
A star-shaped dried spice with a delicate licorice flavor.

Steam or Steaming

Steaming in a bowl can be accomplished by placing an empty tuna can, with the top and bottom removed, in a Dutch oven filled with 2 inches of water. Place bowl on top. Cover and steam.

Taegu

Shredded cuttlefish or cod in a spicy sauce.

Taro Leaves

Also called lu'au leaves, they are similar to spinach leaves in texture and taste.

Tempura

Fish, shrimp or vegetable dipped in a light batter and deep-fried.

Teriyaki

Barbecued or broiled beef or poultry marinated in soy sauce, flavored with ginger, garlic and brown sugar.

Thai Fish Sauce

An anchovy based, dark sauce used to flavor Thai food. Oriental food stores usually carry this.

Ti Leaves

Large smooth green leaves of the ti plant. The leaves are used as "wrappers" for a variety of island dishes.

Tofu

Bean curd or cake, it is white with a custard-like consistency. Usually comes in blocks packed in water.

Ulua

(See fish chart)

Ume Boshi

Unripe plums soaked in brine and packed with red shiso leaves, which flavor and dye the plums pinkish-red.

Wasabi

A hot green horseradish powder used in Japanese cooking. Mix powder with water to form a smooth paste. It may also be called Japanese Green Horseradish. Do not substitute regular horseradish. Wasabi has a very long shelf life.

Water Chestnuts

Crispy, white vegetables covered with a thin, fine, brown-black skin. If fresh, pare before using. If available, they are well worth the effort. Canned, they are readily available.

Wok

Chinese frying pan specifically designed for stir-frying. The shape provides for intense heat at the bottom.

Won Ton

A dumpling made with won ton pi which is filled and deep fried, steamed or cooked soft in soup.

Won Ton Pi

A sheet of pasta dough used to make won ton.

Won Bok

Celery cabbage. A tall, pale green cabbage similar in appearance to romaine lettuce. It has a delicate, mild flavor. Also known as Chinese cabbage.

Hanging
Heliconia

Index

a

b

Bacon
Bacon Dressing **83**
Basic Spinach Salad **68**
Layered Spinach Salad **69**
Spinach Salad with Chutney Dressing **67**

Banana
Banana Cake Waialae Iki **296**
Banana Cow **55**
Banana Lemon Tea Bread **131**
Banana Nut Bread **132**
Coconut Baked Bananas **267**
Coconut Chicken with Fresh Fruit **178**
Cold Banana Bisque with
   Cinnamon Croutons **107**
Fish Divine **188**
Ono Sweet Potatoes **216**
Pele's Bananas **281**
Tropical Nut Bread **133**
Two Crust Banana Pie **304**

Barley
Barley Pilaf **241**

Beans
Eurasian Vegetables **223**
Hidden Palm **221**
Mexican Salad **72**
Portuguese Bean Soup **99**
Portuguese Soup **100**
Prize Winning Chili **154**
Sautéed String Beans and Pork **158**

Bean Sprouts
Bean Sprout Namul **74**

Beef
Beef Tenderloin Stuffed with Lobster **143**
Beef Tomato **142**
Beef with Crisp Long Rice **152**
Classical Korean Dried Beef **149**
Easy Picnic Short Ribs **147**
Filet Charlemagne **144**
Hot Mongolian Beef **150**
Kalbi **148**
Laulau **330**
London Broil **146**
Pine Tree Mushroom Soup **111**
Pipikaula **331**
Pulehu Ribs **146**
Smoked Brisket **147**
Steak Tartare **151**
Tournedos Mitchell **145**
Ground Beef
Baked Stuffed Papaya **153**
Börek **23**
General Poon's Pupu **19**

Hamburger Quiche **232**
Korean Barbecued Hamburgers **148**
Lumpia **21**
Mexican Salad **72**
Prize Winning Chili **154**
Sweet 'N Sour Meatballs **27**

Beverages
Alcoholic
Banana Cow **55**
Blue Hawaii **52**
Bob Nob **56**
Buzz's Golden Coyne **57**
Champagne Punch **54**
État Contente **57**
Henry **53**
Hotel Hana Maui Chi Chi **58**
Kimo's Coconut Pipi **53**
Kimo's Panini **55**
Pink Palace **56**
Volcano in Winter **58**
White Sangria **54**
Wicked Mai Tai Punch **52**
Non-Alcoholic
Grandma Cooke's Iced Tea **59**
Hawaiian Punch **59**
Henrietta **53**
O.C.C. Iced Tea **60**
Tropical Fruit Smoothie **60**
Punch
Champagne Punch **59**
Hawaiian Punch **59**
Wicked Mai Tai Punch **52**

Bran
Icebox Bran Muffins **138**

Breads
Cinnamon Croutons **107**
Crêpe Batter **136**
Garlic Croutons **135**
Gougère **136**
Lavosh **137**
Sunshine Orange Crêpes **127**
Breakfast
Coconut Cinnamon Sour Cream
   Coffee Cake **125**
Dutch Baby **123**
Old-Fashioned Waffles **126**
Quick
Banana Lemon Tea Bread **131**
Banana Nut Bread **132**
Boston Brown Bread **128**
Lemon Bread **134**
Mango Bread **130**
Mmmm Good Mango Bread **129**
Tropical Nut Bread **133**
Zucchini Bread **135**

The Committee

Cherye Pierce and Ann Ellis
Co-Chairmen 1982-83

Carole Wilbur
Chairman 1980-82

Lynn Blakely
Editor

Marianne Dymond
and Pam Gough
Marketing Co-Chairmen

Gretchen Hack,
Lynette Char and Nancy Freeman
Typists

*Committee Members
1982-83*

Diane Ackerson
Coe Atherton
Bambi D'Olier
Sara Dudgeon
Susan Friedl
Sally Habermeyer
Bayanne Hauhart
Liz Howard
Nancy Goessling
Laurie Lawson
Dianne Lee
Carol McNamee
Sally Mist
Chris O'Brien
Kathy Richardson
Debbie Robertson
Sally Schmid
Betty Stickney
Marianne Vaughan

*In any project expertise is a valuable asset.
We would like to give our
special thanks to our experts
for making our job much easier.*

Albert Schmid
Lois Taylor
Bertie Lee
Lila Pang
Margo Stahl
Cleo Evans
Mitch D'Olier
Jean Durkee
Jay Frost
Dee Helber

Contributors

The Junior League of Honolulu would like to thank its members and their families and friends who contributed their recipes, time and creative ideas.

Joan Aanavi
Bob Ackerson
Diane Ackerson
Elizabeth Adams
Corine Albright
Bonnie Andrew
Mary Atchison
Coe Atherton
Lauren Avery
Debra Bauer*
Casey Beck
Mary Ann Bell
Koby Berrington
Constance Black
Cecelia Blackfield
Lynn Blakely
Audrey Bliss
Decie Blitz
Nancy Boyle
Elizabeth Boynton
Joan Bring
Beth Broadbent
Janice Broderick
Jane Burns
Margaret Cameron
Merilyn Cannon
Jean Carlsmith
Jane Carney
Carol Case

Gerry Ching
Philip Ching
Becky Connable
Vivienne Cooke
Mary Cooke
Briar Cornuelle*
Phyllis Corteway
Bee Cromwell*
Dicki Davis
Anita DeDomenico
Diane Dericks
Beth Devereux
Mary Ann Dickie
Bambi D'Olier
Linda Dreher
Sara Dudgeon
Marcia Duff
Margie Durant
Barbara Dwyer
Ann Ellis
Mary Ellis
Marti Erickson
Charlotte Farrell
Patricia Faus
Lesley Ferguson
Connie Flattery
Susan Forman
Pam Freed
Nancy Freeman

Susan Friedl
Lisa Gibson
Trish Glen
Nancy Goessling
Nancy Goodale
Marilyn Goss
Rae Gresso
Lynda Gruver
Sally Habermeyer
Tooty Hager
Leonia Halsey
Renee Hampton
Puddi Hastings
Bayanne Haubart
Patricia Hemmeter
Sue Hendry
Anne Hoadley*
Jeanne Hoffman
Allison Holland
Donna Hoshide
Liz Howard
Mina Humphreys
Helen Hurtig
Patty Inaba
Dana Izumi
Susan Jacobs*
Claire Johnson
Lila Johnson
Margot Johnson

Claire Jones

Jackie Jones

Bonnie Judd

Delores Judd

Sally Judd

Geneal Kanalz

Jean Kellerman

Marie Kelley*

Kristi Kendig

Adrienne King

Hilda Kitagawa

Grace Kobayashi

Mary Kondo

Janet Larsen

Mary Pat Larsen

Tina Lau

Laurie Lawson

Betsy LaTorre

Buzzy Lee

Dianne Lee

Bertie Lee

Mary Lou Lewis

Dee Lum

Cindy Lupton

Teri Machado

Ginny Maciszewski*

Barbara Marumoto

Susan Matthews

Leslie Mattice

Wendy Maxwell

Linda McCabe

Nancy McKibbin

Carol McNamee

Kay McWayne

Peggy Melim

D. C. Mist

Sally Mist

Meredith Moncata

Kaye Moore

Sis Moore

Sharon Morton

Martha Lee Mullen

Margo Mun

Mary Murdy

Teruo Nakama

Pat Neufeldt

Betty Nicholson

Lucille Nimitz

Chris O'Brien

Fran Osborne

Sybil Padgett

Lila Pang

Maggie Parkes

Cherye Pierce

Jim Pierce

Becky Pietsch

Judy Pietsch

Mele Pochevera

Gail Potter

Bonnie Prior

Helja Pruyn

Elizabeth Pump

Mary Richards

Kathy Richardson

Tetta Richert

Jiggs Ritchie

Debbie Robertson

Lei Saito

Mabel Saito

Sally Schmid

Pat Schnack

Bobby Lou Schneider

Sadye Shayer

Dianne Simmons

Donna Singlehurst

Jorgen Skov

Jean Smith

Rebecca Snider-Norris

Diana Snyder

Margo Sorenson

Walton Stansell*

Polly Steiner

Melissa Stevens

Betty Stickney

Paulette Stone*

Mary Anne Stubenberg

Trudie Taylor

Pat Tharp

Susan Thom

Rande Thompkins

Vonnie Turner

Lynn Turner

Marianne Vaughan

Pattie Wagner

Sybil Watson

Lynn Werner

Carolyn Whitney

Carole Wilbur

Norma Wilbur

Mary Wilson

Carolyn Wolfberg

Barbara Wong

Cyndi Wong

Lou Woolley

Kathy Wright

Andy Yim

Eva Zane

*Past Committee Members

The artist

Pegge Hopper, our artist, was born in Oakland, California. She attended the Art Center School in Los Angeles and went east for her first job as a mural designer for Raymond Loewy Associates in New York. There she met her husband Bruce and they married in 1957. They subsequently moved to San Francisco where she free-lanced. Her next move was to Italy where she designed posters and graphics for La Rinascente in Milan. In 1963, she arrived in Honolulu and became art director for Lennen and Newell Advertising Agency for two years. In 1970, she began to paint and print her distinctive island women which are cherished by art collectors. She has had shows in Hawaii and on the mainland and in March of 1983, she opened her own gallery in Honolulu.

In addition to her art accomplishments, Pegge cites her other major project as having three daughters, ages 20, 18 and 7.

The designer

Bruce Hopper, our graphics designer, was born in Los Angeles in 1931. He attended school in Southern California and began free-lance design at the age of sixteen. He received his training at the Art Center in Los Angeles. His subsequent jobs in graphic and industrial design took him to New York, San Francisco, New Canaan, Connecticut and Milan, Italy.

Since moving to Honolulu in 1963, he has created symbols for Hawaiian Telephone, Kapalua Resort, the Honolulu Symphony and many other accounts. He is well known for his store designs and signage projects.

The type

This book was typeset in ITC Garamond, a family of faces copyrighted by the International Typeface Corporation. Created by designer Tony Stan, ITC Garamond is an elegantly updated version of a classic hot metal face. The typography was done by Lettergraphics Memphis.

The Perfect Gift!
• 50,000 copies of "A Taste of Aloha" sold in 24 months
• A wonderful representation of the ethnic diversity of "American" Cuisine

Another Perfect Gift!
"Another Taste of Aloha" is now available! This companion volume to our original cookbook is a contemporary classic that is just the right ingredient for your kitchen library.

Please send me_____ "A Taste of Aloha" cookbooks at $19.95 each   _____
               _____ "Another Taste of Aloha" cookbooks at $19.95 each _____
Postage and handling $3.50 each parcel post   _____
                            $5.00 each air mail   _____
                            Hawaii residents add 4% tax   _____

No C.O.D.s, no foreign checks or currency. Please make checks payable to:
JLH Commercial Publications
Please allow 4-6 weeks for delivery.
Express delivery available on request.

____Payment Enclosed
____Please charge my ☐ VISA ☐ MasterCard

Name: _____

Account #: _____Exp. Date: _____

Telephone, day: (   )_____evening: (   ) _____

Signature:_____

Send to:
Name:_____

Address: _____

City: _____State: _____Zip: _____

Mail or fax this form to:

JUNIOR LEAGUE OF HONOLULU
Commercial Publications Office
1802-A Keeaumoku Street, Honolulu, Hawaii 96822
Fax: (808) 522-0304 Phone: (808) 522-0307

Ask us about other gift ideas.

Prices are subject to change without notice.

Please list any store in your area that might like to handle **A Taste of Aloha**
(name and address)

The Perfect Gift!
• 50,000 copies of "A Taste of Aloha" sold in 24 months
• A wonderful representation of the ethnic diversity of "American" Cuisine

Another Perfect Gift!
"Another Taste of Aloha" is now available! This companion volume to our original cookbook is a contemporary classic that is just the right ingredient for your kitchen library.

Please send me_____ "A Taste of Aloha" cookbooks at $19.95 each _____
_____ "Another Taste of Aloha" cookbooks at $19.95 each _____
Postage and handling $3.50 each parcel post _____
$5.00 each air mail _____
Hawaii residents add 4% tax _____

No C.O.D.s, no foreign checks or currency. Please make checks payable to:
JLH Commercial Publications
Please allow 4-6 weeks for delivery.
Express delivery available on request.

____Payment Enclosed
____Please charge my ☐ VISA ☐ MasterCard

Name: _____

Account #: _____Exp. Date: _____

Telephone, day: (   ) _____evening: (   ) _____

Signature:_____

Send to:
Name:_____

Address: _____

City: _____State: _____Zip: _____

Mail or fax this form to:

JUNIOR LEAGUE OF HONOLULU
Commercial Publications Office
1802-A Keeaumoku Street, Honolulu, Hawaii 96822
Fax: (808) 522-0304   Phone: (808) 522-0307

Ask us about other gift ideas.

Prices are subject to change without notice.

Please list any store in your area that might like to handle **A Taste of Aloha** *(name and address)*

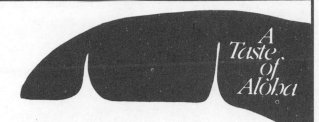

The Perfect Gift!
• 50,000 copies of "A Taste of Aloha" sold in 24 months
• A wonderful representation of the ethnic diversity of "American" Cuisine

Another Perfect Gift!
"Another Taste of Aloha" is now available! This companion volume to our original cookbook is a contemporary classic that is just the right ingredient for your kitchen library.

Please send me_____ "A Taste of Aloha" cookbooks at $19.95 each _____
_____ "Another Taste of Aloha" cookbooks at $19.95 each _____
Postage and handling $3.50 each parcel post   _____
$5.00 each air mail   _____
Hawaii residents add 4% tax   _____

No C.O.D.s, no foreign checks or currency. Please make checks payable to:
JLH Commercial Publications
Please allow 4-6 weeks for delivery.
Express delivery available on request.

____Payment Enclosed
____Please charge my   ☐ VISA   ☐ MasterCard

Name: _____

Account #: _____Exp. Date: _____

Telephone, day: (   ) _____evening: (   ) _____

Signature:_____

Send to:
Name:_____

Address: _____

City: _____State: _____Zip: _____

Mail or fax this form to:

JUNIOR LEAGUE OF HONOLULU
Commercial Publications Office
1802-A Keeaumoku Street, Honolulu, Hawaii 96822
Fax: (808) 522-0304 Phone: (808) 522-0307

Ask us about other gift ideas.

Prices are subject to change without notice.

Please list any store in your area that might like to handle **A Taste** of **Aloha**
(name and address)

The Perfect Gift!

• 50,000 copies of "A Taste of Aloha" sold in 24 months
• A wonderful representation of the ethnic diversity of "American" Cuisine

Another Perfect Gift!

"Another Taste of Aloha" is now available! This companion volume to our original cookbook is a contemporary classic that is just the right ingredient for your kitchen library.

Please send me_____ "A Taste of Aloha" cookbooks at $19.95 each _____
_____ "Another Taste of Aloha" cookbooks at $19.95 each _____
Postage and handling $3.50 each parcel post _____
   $5.00 each air mail _____
   Hawaii residents add 4% tax _____

No C.O.D.s, no foreign checks or currency. Please make checks payable to:
JLH Commercial Publications
Please allow 4-6 weeks for delivery.
Express delivery available on request.

_____Payment Enclosed
_____Please charge my ☐ VISA ☐ MasterCard

Name: _____

Account #: _____ Exp. Date: _____

Telephone, day: ( ) _____ evening: ( ) _____

Signature: _____

Send to:
Name: _____

Address: _____

City: _____ State: _____ Zip: _____

Mail or fax this form to:

JUNIOR LEAGUE OF HONOLULU
Commercial Publications Office
1802-A Keeaumoku Street, Honolulu, Hawaii 96822
Fax: (808) 522-0304 Phone: (808) 522-0307

Ask us about other gift ideas.

Prices are subject to change without notice.

Please list any store in your area that might like to handle **A Taste of Aloha**
(name and address)